GENDER, UNPAID LABOR,
AND THE PROMOTION OF LITERACY

GARLAND REFERENCE LIBRARY
OF SOCIAL SCIENCE
(Vol. 401)

GENDER, UNPAID LABOR, AND THE PROMOTION OF LITERACY
A Selected, Annotated Bibliography

Cheryl Knott Malone

GARLAND PUBLISHING, INC. • NEW YORK & LONDON
1987

© 1987 Cheryl Knott Malone
All rights reserved

Library of Congress Cataloging-in-Publication Data

Malone, Cheryl Knott, 1954–
Gender, Unpaid Labor, and the Promotion of Literacy.

(Garland Reference Library of Social Science;
vol. 401)
Includes indexes.
1. Volunteer workers in education—United States—
Bibliography.   2. Volunteer workers in libraries—
United States—Bibliography.   3. Voluntarism—United
States—Bibliography.   4. Literacy—United States—
Bibliography.   5. Sexual division of labor—United
States—Bibliography.   I. Title.   II. Series: Garland
Reference Library of Social Science; v. 401.

Z7164.V65M34   1987   [LB2844.1.V6]   016.3613'7   87-25753
ISBN 0–8240–8469–1 (alk. paper)

Printed on acid-free, 250-year-life paper
Manufactured in the United States of America

To Paul

CONTENTS

Preface. ix

The Gender Dimension of Literacy
     Volunteer Work. xiii

Bibliography 1

Author Index 115

Title Index 123

Subject Index. 143

PREFACE

   Cited in this bibliography are materials on volunteers in schools, libraries, after-school programs, higher education, and literacy campaigns. Selected English-language books, articles, government publications, and doctoral dissertations produced in the United States are included.
   Chronological arrangement, with entries in alphabetical order within years, makes explicit certain historical trends. For instance, the relative scarcity of literature about volunteers in education until the late 1950s made it possible to group the early readings together. Beginning with 1960, each year constitutes a separate division. The author, title, and subject indexes at the end provide alternative access points to each listing.
   All annotations are based on the compiler's inspection of the material. In cases where the original was consulted but has also been reproduced on *Educational Resources Information Center (ERIC)* microfiche, the citation supplies the ERIC Document number. When gender, race, or age inform a particular work, the annotation reflects that perspective. Notes also describe photographs that accompany articles; language may obfuscate gender and race, but visual images do not.
   Volunteer programs in religious organizations and vocational-technical schools are not included. Also left out are volunteers serving differently abled persons including those with physical, mental, and emotional handicaps; gifted and exceptional children; adults learning English as a second language; and computer literacy efforts.
   Literacy has a fairly broad construction, encompassing mastery of reading, writing, and arithmetic sufficient for everyday living. The notion of literacy promotion includes not only volunteers directly involved in tutoring but also those generally supporting through their unwaged labor the work of schools and libraries. Such support at bottom serves the literacy cause. Volunteer programs and projects in schools, for

children and adults, in libraries, and outside these institutions are covered. Because of the repetition of themes and approaches in the education and library literature, this bibliography represents patterns, perspectives, and concerns apparent in the written record rather than listing comprehensively. Additionally, it includes works that do not mention gender explicitly but that serve to enhance the reader's grasp of the contribution and place of volunteers and their labors.

Sources searched for the 1946 through 1986 period included the *Education Index* and the *Monthly Catalog of Government Publications*. The birth of ERIC in 1966 made accessible, through *Resources in Education (RIE)*, many local reports and documents that otherwise would have been lost to the researcher. The existence of RIE may account somewhat for the increasing volume of materials after the mid-1960s.

An online search of *Dissertation Abstracts International*, conducted at Eastern Michigan University with help from the Reference staff, proved fruitful. Many of the dissertations contain excellent bibliographies, from which some of the citations here are taken. Because a bibliography is intended to increase access, dissertations housed at institutions that decline to lend them and those available only through purchase are not cited.

Book titles came from the *Library of Congress Catalog Books: Subjects* and from subject searches of the card catalogs at the University of Arizona, University of Michigan, and Eastern Michigan University Libraries. Generally, multiple editions of a title are not included unless they reveal a significant shift in the author's view or add substantial new information.

The reading lists appended to the consulted books, dissertations, and articles yielded more items, including the few newspaper and popular magazine stories cited.

Readers interested in the overall development of volunteer labor and in ideas about the management of unpaid workers will find many sources of information in this list. These materials also indicate the variety of settings for and tasks of volunteers. "Volunteer workers in education" and "volunteer workers in libraries," especially after the mid-1960s, proved to be useful subject headings. Earlier, "volunteer service" and "volunteer assistants" yielded works on unpaid labor in schools and libraries.

Those studying the history of particular groups or programs can begin gathering background material here, then go on to search under more specific subject headings, such as "Friends of the Library," "Literacy Volunteers of America," or "Parent-Teacher Association." Persons seeking to understand public policy affecting volunteer work will find references herein to the Elementary and Secondary Education Act, the Library Services and Construction Act, and other legislation.

Additional sources to check include Marianne Ferber's *Women and Work, Paid and Unpaid: A Selected, Annotated Bibliography* (Garland, 1986) and Doris B. Gold's *Opposition to Volunteerism: An Annotated Bibliography* (CPL Bibliographies, 1979).

During the process of gathering these materials, the interlibrary loan services at the University of Michigan and University of Arizona Libraries were extremely helpful. I visited the Tucson, Houston, Detroit, and Ann Arbor Public Libraries as well. The University of Michigan routinely makes available to its faculty, students, and staff convenient computer facilities, which eased my task.

My gratitude goes to Karen Anderson for her conviction that the study of volunteer workers is an important part of women's history and to Donald Dickinson, who set me on the bibliographic course. I also appreciate John Price-Wilkin's technical advice.

THE GENDER DIMENSION
OF LITERACY VOLUNTEER WORK

Research into the promotion of literacy presents an opportunity for contemplating volunteerism and its meaning in our society. It also focuses on sex roles, since most individual promoters of literacy have been women, working with or without pay as teachers, tutors, and librarians. Consequently, the study of women laboring to produce literate citizens can reveal our culture's attitudes toward work, education, social service, professionalism, volunteerism, class, and race--and the gender dimension of each. By concentrating on the forty years after World War Two, it is possible to trace the development of volunteerism as a response to particular circumstances which changed over time.

For instance, the "teacher-moms" of the 1950s devoted hours of unpaid labor in the private and public spheres on behalf of their children. In the 1960s, the impact of President Johnson's War on Poverty and the Civil Rights Movement became apparent, when college students and community activists saw literacy tutoring as one solution to the problems of disadvantaged minorities. Later, the criticism of volunteerism during the second wave of feminism in the 1970s gave way to the Reagan rhetoric of reliance on the private sector in the 1980s. Throughout, a common theme underlay the discussion: the realization that public education consistently failed to impart the ability to read, write, and perform basic calculations in a significant percentage of its constituents.

The end of World War Two marked the end of a long period of deprivation, Americans found themselves free to consume again, and the economy grew tremendously. Within that growth an important shift occurred; by the middle of the 1950s, the service sector had begun to outdistance heavy industry as the primary source of employment. At the same time, the population boom forced the public school system to accommodate increasing numbers of new students. In hospitals and in education, women workers predominated; in both areas volunteers became integral to the provision of services.

    The institutionalization of volunteer work after World War Two began in the health care industry. A manual published by the American Hospital Association in 1944 declared that "circumstances related to World War Two have brought about far-reaching changes. Volunteer service is no longer confined to a few hospitals, but it has found a place as a necessary supplement to the hospital's highly trained professional personnel throughout the country." (1) Administrators and trustees hoped they would stay in peacetime, with its remarkable population boom and economic growth. The federal government sponsored hospital construction, a neglected activity during the Depression and War, while at the same time the supply of nurses dwindled. By 1947, the American Hospital Association had added a separate division devoted to volunteer activities, and by 1950, an estimated half-million women were working without pay in hospitals. By 1964, that figure had quadrupled. Health care volunteerism became a model for educators, and remained so into the 1980s. (2)

    The first full-blown school volunteer program began in New York City in the latter 1950s. Initially a pilot project sponsored by the Public Education Association with private foundation support and the approval of the Board of Education, it later became part of the Board's regular budget. It also became a model for the incorporation of unpaid labor in the schools. Within the next decade, the Public Education Association had acquired a Ford Foundation grant to establish the National School Volunteer Program to encourage volunteer work in schools across the country. (3)

    Part of the impetus behind the volunteer idea was a perceived teacher shortage and the coincident move toward "differentiated staffing," the introduction of teacher's assistants into the classroom. In the early stage of this development, it was seldom clear whether aides should be paid. Often paid and volunteer aides

Introduction　　　　　　　　　　　　　　　　　　　xv

performed the same or similar duties side by side. Teachers also began to turn to older students to tutor younger ones, claiming it benefited both groups. (4)

Additionally, the library profession had failed to attain consensus on the need for libraries in every public school and trained librarians in every library. Mothers started many a school library with nothing more than conviction and a donated collection. School librarians turned to pupil assistants as well as a source of unwaged labor. (5)

This long-standing dependence on volunteers demonstrates that the "taxpayers' revolt" of the 1970s was not unique to that era. Many educators habitually used the rhetoric of retrenchment to express their frustration over chronically tight budgets. The availability of volunteers sometimes made possible the channeling of dollars away from schools to other city or county services. At other times, lack of funds forced administrators to turn to unpaid workers to staff classrooms and libraries. (6)

At the same time that education administrators were experimenting with volunteer work in the schools, others began to address the problem of illiterate adults. In the 1950s the Adult Education Association and the United States Office of Education founded the National Commission for Adult Literacy to collect data, increase the public's awareness of the problem of illiteracy, and establish a central clearing house for the exchange of information. (7)

Yet the schools continued to turn out illiterate students every year. Because many volunteers worked outside the formal educational system, their presence represented a critique of the method that failed so many of its constituents. Such programs targeted not only the children needing extra attention in classrooms, but also their parents and their younger siblings. In 1962, Ruth Colvin established Literacy Volunteers of America, a private organization matching trained volunteer tutors to illiterate adult students. Six years later, the international organization Laubach Literacy spun

off a United States group, the National
Affiliation for Literacy Advance.
     The ferment of the sixties led to a
reconceptualization of illiteracy within the
context of poverty. Writers began to call for the
expansion of the volunteer labor force, claiming
that white, middle-class women and businessmen were
overrepresented. Government programs, such as
Project Head Start, required community
participation, which often translated into
volunteer work by participating children's
mothers. ACTION established the National Student
Volunteer Program in 1967, attempting to funnel
high school and college students' energies into
socially acceptable volunteer work. Alternatives
to classroom instruction developed at the
instigation of volunteers, with after-school
programs in inner-city Chicago as the prototype.
(9)
     By the time the federal government undertook
its first nationwide survey of volunteers, women's
unpaid labor was institutionalized in a pattern
determined by and reflective of the sexual
division of paid labor. The government survey,
conducted in 1965, documented that the "typical"
volunteer was a married, white woman between
twenty-five and forty-four years old with a high
school diploma. Excluding religious activities,
her most frequent volunteer experience was as a
Girl Scout leader, a teacher's aide, or both.
Almost sixty percent of the 6.7 million volunteers
in nonreligious work were women. Among the men
who did volunteer work, eighteen percent engaged
in educational programs, as compared to thirty-
four percent of the women volunteers. The most
popular secular arenas for women's volunteer work
were, in order, educational services, social or
welfare work, and hospitals, all traditionally
reserved for women workers. (10) Depending on the
times and the prevailing notions about where
illiterates were likely to exist, all three arenas
were potential sites for volunteers to provide
reading instruction.
     Consequently, the feminist critique of
volunteer service as exploitive of women occurred
at the historical moment when social institutions,

Introduction xvii

including the government, seemed most intent on entrenching women in a never-ending round of unwaged work. The National Organization for Women in 1971 issued a statement advocating women's activism but decrying their contribution of volunteer services. *Ms.* magazine covered the issue in 1975, reprinting the NOW position paper and launching a debate that many pro-volunteer writers thereafter felt compelled to acknowledge. (11)
    In fact, and for a variety of reasons, married women and mothers, long the pool from which to draw volunteers, began seeking paid employment in record numbers. Administrators engaged in the promotion of literacy stepped up efforts to recruit nontraditional volunteers. Older children were recruited to tutor younger; college students were encouraged on the grounds that it would give them marketable skills and meaningful experiences; and older Americans were targeted with the assurance that they still had much to give. Nevertheless, women remained the key contributors of unpaid work.
    In effect, volunteers subsidized both a system that was ineffective for millions of its constituents and the auxiliaries of and alternatives to that system.
    Women have always labored without pay, but not until the post-World War Two period has that labor systematically been rationalized, bureaucratized, and institutionalized. Literacy promotion--in public schools, grassroots programs, and libraries--has attempted to take advantage of that development. Education is a natural place to begin the study of gender, volunteerism, and the promotion of literacy. Such a topic, with its interdisciplinary ramifications, suggests numerous explorations.
    For example, it is probably no coincidence that hospitals, schools, and libraries--with predominately female labor forces--were prime candidates for volunteerism. For some women, it may have been a short leap from low pay to no pay, especially if by sacrificing salaries they gained flexible working hours and perhaps some prestige. They could lead an essentially private life while

periodically participating in the public sphere. But what of the women who worked for pay--teachers and librarians among them--and who saw the introduction of volunteers as a threat to job security and decent salaries? A close study of the social relations between paid and unpaid workers could lead to a clearer understanding of women's economic status.

Volunteers' interactions with each other and with their charges are ripe for study as well. One-to-one tutoring provided the opportunity to form intense, interdependent relationships between, for instance, middle-class women and working-class men or white women and black. Moving portrayals of illiterate adults who struggle to learn obliterate another side of the illiteracy story: women in schools, libraries, private homes, and neighborhood centers recruiting each other, managing each other, evaluating each other, and laboriously encouraging the students who escaped the lessons of the educational system.

It seems important also to document the actual contributions women's unpaid work has made to the educational system. Such an approach necessarily takes the institution's perspective, and should be balanced by the volunteer's. Why did she do it? Why did she stop? Certainly, one feature of the housewife's time spent in volunteer services was its peculiar function as organized, supervised "leisure" activity.

The role of government as chief volunteerism booster represents another avenue for exploration. It may be fruitful to ask whether Head Start programs might have been different had women not already demonstrated willingness to contribute their labor as well as tax dollars for social programs. Had women's unwaged work not been an option, the entire War on Poverty might have been organized differently. Such research may lead to conclusions regarding the ways in which government policies shape volunteer work and structure gender roles.

Finally, a careful study of the debate regarding whether women's volunteer work is exploitive would reveal a gerat deal not only about economic issues but also about the state of

Introduction xix

the women's movement from the early 1970s to the present.

Nothing is more indicative of the conflict than the 1984 publication of Wendy Kaminer's book on volunteerism as a positive force in women's lives. (12) In fact, Kaminer's work culminated the argument against NOW's position which had become commonplace in introductions to books about volunteering. Here, then, was a self-proclaimed feminist arguing that the distinction between activism and service volunteering was ambiguous as well as self-serving on the part of middle-class, white feminists.

Still, NOW set the terms and tone of the debate and subsequent writers have failed to transcend them. Research reported in a scholarly fashion might be able to work through the arguments and set a new framework for discussion. Perhaps such a study could start from the assumption that the point is not service versus activist volunteerism or paid versus unpaid work, but whether women and men were enervated or empowered by their labors in the forty years since the end of World War Two.

NOTES

1. American Hospital Association. *Organization Guide for Hospital Volunteer Service* (Chicago: American Hospital Association, 1944), p. 1.
2. Arden, Eugene. "Using Volunteers: Colleges Can Learn from Hospitals." *The Chronicle of Higher Education* 63 (July 1986): 613.
3. Tunick, Adele B. "Volunteer Services for Schools." *Scholastic Teacher* 87 (October 21, 1965): 10.
4. Shipp, Mary E. "Teacher Adies: A Survey." *The National Elementary Principal* 46 (May 1967): 30-3; Stouffer, Russell G., and Patrick Groff. "Should You Use Pupil Tutors?" *Instructor* 77 (August-September 1967): 35.
5. Douglas, Mary Peacock. *The Pupil Assistant in the School Library.* Chicago: American Library Association, 1957.
6. Harmer, Ruth Mulvey. "Three R's and an S for Service." *Reader's Digest*, January 1957, pp. 150-2; Troutner, Joan, and Norma Musar. "Parent Aides for Public Kindergarten ... A Pilot Project." *Arizona Teacher* 56 (May 1968): 16-8.
7. Caliver, Ambrose. "For a More Literate Nation." *School Life* 40 (December 1957): 13-4.
8. Cohen, Royce. "Partners for Literacy." *American Education* 6 (June 1970): 36; Jones, Edward V. *Reading Instruction for the Adult Illiterate* (Chicago: American Library Association, 1981), p. 19.
9. Caplin, Morris D. "An Invaluable Resource: The School Volunteer." *Clearing House* 45 (September 1970): 10-4; Janowitz, Gayle. "After-School Study Centers: Volunteer Work in Reading." Bethesda, Maryland: ERIC Document Reproduction Service, ED 001751, 1964.
10. U.S. Department of Labor. Manpower Administration. *Americans Volunteer.* Manpower/Automation Research Monograph No. 10. (Washington, D.C.: Government Printing Office, 1969), p. 3.
11. The *Ms.* series begins on page 70 of the February 1975 issue with an editorial by Gloria Steinem, "Volunteerism: Your Money or Your Life?"
12. Kaminer, Wendy. *Women Volunteering: The Pleasure, Pain, and Politics of Unpaid Work from 1830 to the Present.* Garden City, NY: Anchor Press, 1984.

Gender, Unpaid Labor,
and the Promotion of Literacy

1946-1959

1. Anderson, Betty; Mary E. Crawford; Pearl Osborne; and Gordon Klopf. "Becoming Community Participants." *Journal of Higher Education* 27 (May 1956): 276-9.

    A how-to piece on incorporating college students as volunteers in social service agencies.

2. Atkins, Martin, and Bruce Fiandt. "Teachers for a Day." *School Executive* 74 (March 1955): 88-9.

    Advocates allowing parent-volunteers to replace teachers for a day to allow parents to experience classroom problems first-hand.

3. Bloom, Murray Teigh. "Need Help on Those Local 'Drives'? Enlist the Teens!" *Rotarian* 82 (March 1953): 18-21.

    Describes programs to involve high-school students in volunteer activities in Baltimore and elsewhere.

4. Boutwell, W.D. "What's Happening in Education? Teachers Aides." *National Parent-Teacher* 49 (January 1954): 13.

    Reports briefly on the use of parent volunteers to lessen teachers' workloads.

5. Brown, George W. "No Trained Teachers for Foreign Languages?" *Nation's Schools* 55 (March 1955): 53.

    Describes a Mamaroneck, New York, public school's use of volunteers to teach German, French, and Spanish because of paid teachers' insufficient training. A young mother with a Ph.D. in Romance languages prepared lesson plans in each language.

6. Cortright, Richard W. "They Are Learning to Read." *Adult Leadership* 8 (June 1959): 54-6.

Maintains that government alone cannot help ten million illiterate Americans and insists on the need for immediate training of volunteer teachers. Recounts the efforts of the Baylor Literacy Center and the Abilene (Texas) Woman's Club to prepare tutors.

7. Douglas, Mary Peacock. *The Pupil Assistant in the School Library*. Chicago: American Library Association, 1957.

Provides guidance for school librarians using volunteer students as staff. Part II reproduces application and evaluation forms, a handbook for assistants, and recruitment fliers.

8. Fontaine, Andre. "School's More Fun When Parents Help Teach." *Reader's Digest*, March 1950, pp. 126-8. (Condensed from the September 1949 issue of *National Parent-Teacher*.)

Describes how volunteer men and women introduce students in Long Island schools to geography, jobs, and hobbies.

9. Harmer, Ruth Mulvey. "Three R's and an S for Service." *Reader's Digest*, January 1957, pp. 150-2.

Notes that Hollywood (California) High School's budget "is never quite equal to its responsibilities" and advocates the use of student volunteers to aid teachers, answer the switchboard, and act as lifeguards.

10. Hawkins, Thomas E. "Volunteer Tutorial System." *Phi Delta Kappan* 40 (January 1959): 168-9.

Advocates engaging gifted male students as tutors for struggling underclassmen.

11. Hickey, Margaret. "When Migrant Children Arrive ... Volunteers Are There to Help." *Ladies Home Journal*, January 1957, p. 21.

Portrays the American Association of University Women summer school for children of migrant farmworkers in Illinois, including AAUW's assertion that as U.S. citizens, the children deserve public-school education. Notes that limited funds make that unlikely.

12. Logan, George King. "Volunteers--For Publicity." *Louisiana Library Association Bulletin* 10 (March 1947): 72-4.

Traces the origin of volunteer work in the New Orleans Public Library to World War Two's Civil Defense Volunteer Office and the library's need for staff to compile and distribute war-related information. Counsels against recruiting individuals not affiliated with such organizations as the Council of Jewish Women and the Junior League to avoid giving the impression that volunteers compete with paid workers for specific jobs.

13. Long, Helen Halter. "What Price Parent Participation?" *National Elementary Principal* 37 (September 1956): 132-8.

Accounts from four Marmaroneck, New York, school principals of volunteers, how they overcame teacher opposition, and how they produce positive publicity.

14. Peckham, Earl K. "Volunteer Work--Its Relation to Education." *School and Society* 64 (October 12, 1946): 261-2.

Emphasizes that students should become volunteers, thereby continuing the spirit of service evident during war.

15. Phinney, Eleanor. *Library Adult Education in Action: Five Case Studies*. Chicago: American Library Association, 1956.

Argues the centrality of volunteers to adult services because they represent community involvement in programming. All five of the libraries studied used volunteers.

16. Wood, W. R. "Community Responsibility for Literacy Education." *School Life* 34 (November 1951): 23.

Asserts that community involvement must support local school boards' programs to eradicate illiteracy. Also acknowledges that because there are seldom enough volunteers available to handle all facets of a literacy program, local, state, and federal governments must commit resources as well. The third of four articles in a series on illiteracy suggested by the Office of Education Committee on Educational Rejectees.

1960

17. Berg, Paul Conrad. "Illiteracy at the Crossroads." *Adult Leadership* 9 (June 1960): 47-8.

Describes attempts to eradicate illiteracy in the South via broadcast media and volunteer facilitators.

18. Trasin, Walter. "Can Learners Teach?" *Clearing House* 34 (January 1960): 263-5.

Advocates use of students as teachers because their lack of adult authoritarianism frees students to ask probing questions and thereby learn more.

19. Wright, Benjamin. "News and Comment: Should Children Teach?" *Elementary School Journal* 60 (April 1960): 353-69.

Asserts that children should be used as volunteer aides and tutors because early teaching experiences help convince them to become paid teachers later.

1961

20. Jamer, T. Margaret. *School Volunteers: Creating a New Dimension in Education Through Lay Participation: Including the History of the First School Volunteer Program.* New York: Public Education Association, 1961.

Traces the history of the New York City School Volunteers program begun in 1956. Includes photographs shot by a school volunteer photographer depicting exclusively women as volunteers.

21. Pines, Maya. "Little Extra Push: School Volunteer Program." *Reporter* 24 (March 16, 1961): 37-8.

Describes the volunteer work of individual women involved in the New York City School Volunteer Program.

1962

22. "A Season of Helping." *Time*, August 10, 1962, p. 28.

Surveys a smattering of summertime volunteer work of college and high school students, including tutoring of black dropouts in Chicago.

1963

23. Delaney, Arthur A. "Good Students Help Deficient Pupils." *School Activities* 35 (October 1963): 36.

Suggests encouraging National Honor Society members to set up after-school tutoring.

24. The President's Commission on the Status of Women. *Four Consultations*. Washington, D.C.: Government Printing Office, 1963.

One of the four consultations covers "New Patterns in Volunteer Work." The Commission's committees on home and community and on education did not question volunteerism, but sought new ways for the public sector to train and use volunteers.

25. Swanker, Esther M. "On the Care and Feeding of Volunteers." *Library Journal* 88 (April 15, 1963): 1728-9.

Takes exception to library standards that approve of volunteer labor as a stopgap measure only; advocates the use of mothers throughout the year in two-hour shifts.

1964

26. Brentlinger, Howard R. "Volunteer Services at the Cornell Public Library." *The Bookmark* 23 (July 1964): 292-4.

Declares that professional librarians and volunteers can work together, with unpaid staff performing technical services and clerical tasks. Boasts that wives of both professional men and Cornell faculty members serve as volunteers.

27. Fontaine, Andre. "The Remarkable Story of the Dropouts and the College Students." *McCall's*, March 1964, p. 36.

Reports on the development of the Northern Student Movement whose white, college-age members provide free tutoring for mostly urban black students.

28. Janowitz, Gayle. "After-School Study Centers: Volunteer Work in Reading." Bethesda, Maryland: ERIC Document Reproduction Service, ED 001751, 1964.

A thoughtful account of experiences at a volunteer-staffed after-school center serving disadvantaged children in Chicago's Hyde Park neighborhood. The final chapter outlines rules for volunteers and includes the suggestion that they keep their cigarettes and money out of sight when they work at the center.

Promotion of Literacy 7

29. "Student Tutors for Floundering Classmates."
School Activities 35 (April 1964): 255-6.

Describes how the all-male New Jersey high school Key Club initiated after-school tutoring programs which later enlisted help from members of the Future Teachers Club.

30. "Volunteers Sought for Literacy Drive." *New York Times*, January 13, 1964, p. 13.

Announces commitment by labor unions, churches, and civil rights groups to recruit volunteers for Laubach training as literacy tutors.

1965

31. Baun, Eugene L. "The Washington University Campus Y Tutoring Project." *Peabody Journal of Education* 43 (November 1965): 161-8.

Describes literacy and subject tutoring provided in the all-black city of Kinloch, near St. Louis, Missouri, to remedy the lack of materials and teachers in the poverty-stricken area.

32. Burkhardt, Ann Strayer. "The Trained Volunteer and the Elementary Library." *American School Board Journal* 150 (March 1965): 15-6.

Description of the work of mother-volunteers in Darien, Connecticut, school libraries, where the local board of education could not afford to hire professional librarians.

33. Cortright, Richard W. "Profile of a Literacy Teacher." *Adult Education* 15 (Spring 1965): 167-72.

Includes statistics from surveys of participants in Literacy Workshops of the

Washington, D.C., Literacy Council during 1963; eighty-three percent of those surveyed were women.

34. Fresno City Unified School District. "Using Volunteers in Compensatory Education." Bethesda, Maryland, 1965. ED 001461.

Includes a statement regarding the needs of disadvantaged students and the skills volunteers should display. Reproduces sample volunteer application form.

35. Freund, Janet. "Time and Knowledge to Share." *Elementary School Journal* 65 (April 1965): 351-8.

Depicts a Winnetka, Illinois, program to help underachieving boys who--because most teachers are women--lack male role models. A model of sex-role socialization, the program involved businessmen, including the retired and semiretired, who talked about their work experiences with first- through fifth-graders.

36. Hawkins, Thomas E. "Utilizing the Services of the Academically Talented Students." *Journal of Negro Education* 34 (Winter 1965): 93-5.

Argues that volunteer tutors can give college freshmen a sense of belonging and prevent them from dropping out.

37. Janowitz, Gayle. *Helping Hands: Volunteer Work in Education*. Chicago: The University of Chicago Press, 1965.

Focuses on helping disadvantaged students by setting up after-school reading programs staffed by volunteers. Includes compelling accounts of black and Hispanic children referred to the programs. Front cover features a picture of a man teaching a boy to read, but Janowitz acknowledges the scarcity of male volunteers.

38. Lee, Calvin B. T. "The Columbia College Citizenship Program." *Journal of Higher Education* 36 (April 1965): 186-94.

    Describes the unpaid work of Columbia and Barnard students at hospitals, community centers, public schools, government offices, and psychiatric institutions.

39. McCracken, Robert A.; Berniece Leaf; and Laura Johnson. "Individualizing Reading with Pupil-Teachers." *Education* 86 (November 1965): 174-6.

    Suggests that even when there is no money to purchase books, seventh-graders can be induced to write stories for and teach reading to second- and third-grade "reluctant readers."

40. Newton, Eunice Shaed. "Training the Volunteer Reading Tutor." *Journal of Reading* 8 (January 1965): 169-74.

    Description, syllabus and outline of content of a ten-hour course for literacy volunteers in Washington, D.C.

41. Norton, Eloise. "School Libraries and Volunteer Help." *Peabody Journal of Education* 43 (July 1965): 18-20.

    Recounts the work of thirty-four volunteers in seventeen Houston elementary schools, including circulation, story time, shelving, and other duties.

42. Roedder, Kathleen R. "The PTA--Library Supporter." *Instructor* 75 (November 1965): 83.

    Recommends that mothers establish elementary and secondary school libraries, work toward the employment of professional librarians, and willingly submit to professional supervision when paid librarians are hired.

43. Sleisenger, Lenore. *Guidebook for the Volunteer Reading Teacher.* New York: Teachers College Press, 1965.

Addresses volunteers who teach reading to "socially disadvantaged" children in the belief that the unpaid worker's best feature is the conviction that the child is capable of learning. Includes suggestions regarding the organization of lessons, methods, and materials, and special activities. Provides a short list of books appropriate for children with reading problems.

44. "Ten Proven Programs to Prevent Dropouts." *School Management* 9 (October 1965): 70-4.

Outlines Cornell University students' tutoring of high school students and their plans to expand by recruiting women volunteers from the local community.

45. Tunick, Adele B. "Volunteer Services for Schools; National School Volunteer Program." *Scholastic Teacher* 87 (October 21, 1965): 10.

Describes the National School Volunteer Program and its goals including "to relieve the professional staff of non-instructional duties." One accompanying photograph depicts a female volunteer and another shows male and female graduate students as volunteers.

46. Willey, Lawrence. "Reading in High Gear." *Wilson Library Bulletin* 40 (September 1965): 61.

Describes a literacy program which includes instructor's manuals geared toward volunteer tutors. A photograph shows a white boy helping a black girl with a textbook.

47. Wright, Elizabeth J. "Upper-graders Learn by Teaching." *Instructor* 75 (October 1965): 102-3.

Declares that younger children's school work improves with tutoring because they admire their tutors as older brothers and sisters. Four pictures show both boys and girls in teaching and learning roles.

1966

48. "Administrators' Forum--Readers' Choice." *School Management* 10 (January 1966): 84-7.

Presents a case study approach for handling a principal who refuses to allow volunteers in classrooms. One respondent suggests that performance standards be established prior to introducing volunteers into the work setting; another argues that pay commands allegiance and control.

49. MacDonald, Bernice. *Literacy Activities in Public Libraries: A Report of a Study of Services to Adult Illiterates*. Chicago: American Library Association, 1966.

Mentions the role of volunteers in some of the programs described.

50. Mallery, D. "Something More." *Saturday Review*, June 18, 1966, 70-1.

Reports on the variety of tasks engaging older student volunteers, citing tutoring as the most fulfilling. One photograph shows two male volunteers with four younger male students; another depicts a white female volunteer with a younger black female student.

51. Perkins, Bryce. *Getting Better Results from Substitutes, Teacher Aides, and Volunteers*. Englewood Cliffs, New Jersey: Prentice-Hall, 1966.

Credits the Head Start program with encouraging an influx of volunteer workers in education in 1965. Recommends recruiting paid and unpaid aides from the same pool of housewives, mothers, and grandmothers.

52. Petgen, Elizabeth A. "Inside to Outside and Back Again." *Southeastern Librarian* 16 (Summer 1966): 107-12.

   Discusses participation of such organizations as the Junior League, American Association of University Women, and the YWCA in providing volunteers for preschool story hours in Charlotte and Mecklenberg, North Carolina, libraries. Notes the importance of the only male volunteer to the children. A photo shows three women volunteers.

53. Shalen, Marcia. "The School Volunteer Program." Bethesda, Maryland: ERIC Document Reproduction Service, ED 010743, 1966.

   Reports on a pilot project begun in 1965 which demonstrated the value of volunteers and attracted the support of the Ford Foundation, eventually spawning similar projects in twenty large U.S. cities. Stresses the importance of careful screening and training.

54. Shue, D. E. "Adult Literacy Classes in Public Library." *Southeastern Librarian* 16 (Summer 1966): 98-100.

   Describes racially integrated literacy classes in the Cumberland County Public Library of Fayetteville, North Carolina, sponsored in the early 1960s by a sorority and a women's club until the community college system took over adult education activities in the state.

55. Watman, Thomas J. "The Youthful Revolution in Puddledock." *School Activities* 37 (April 1966): 11-2.

   Argues that communities can avoid the problem of adolescent rebellion by channeling teenagers' energies into unpaid labor; describes a high school program with five hundred student volunteers.

1967

56. Boyles, Beatrice C. "New Branches Grow on the Educational Family Tree." *National Elementary Principal* 45 (May 1967): 38-9.

    Asserts that the use of paid and unpaid paraprofessionals decreases teachers' duties by thirty percent and magnifies teacher prestige. Focuses on the principal's leadership in incorporating paraprofessionals into the classroom.

57. Brain, Joseph J. "The Role of the Volunteer." *Adult Leadership* 16 (June 1967): 57.

    Recounts statistics from the Literacy Council survey of volunteers and summarizes the activities of some programs in the Washington, D.C. area.

58. Cardenas, Joe A.; James A. Forester; and Patricia A. Graham. "College Students Become Teachers' Helpers." *Texas Outlook* 51 (May 1967): 56-7.

    Argues that volunteers relieve teachers of clerical duties, but then describes volunteers working with students, compiling bibliographies, grading papers, and preparing science experiments.

59. Educational Service Bureau, Inc. *Working with Children Individually: A Handbook for School Volunteers and Auxiliary Staff*. Arlington, Virginia: The Bureau, 1967.

    Notes that the U.S. Office of Education encourages use of volunteers. Addresses volunteers directly; states their purpose is to provide one-to-one attention to schoolchildren.

60. Gittelson, Natalie. "Second Pair of Hands: School Volunteer Program." *New York Times Magazine,* March 19, 1967, p. 104. Discussion April 9, p. 100, and April 16, p. 22.

Notes the importance of homemakers whose children have left home as a source of unpaid labor for New York schools. Letters in response to the article provide differing perspectives, but none questions the validity of feminine volunteerism.

61. Hiatt, Peter, and Henry T. Drennan, eds. *Public Library Services for the Functionally Illiterate: A Survey of Practice*. Chicago: American Library Association, 1967.

    Responses of three hundred public libraries reveal use of volunteers as tutors and to conduct Spanish-language story hours.

62. Hillenbrand, Robert F. "An Elementary Principal Views the Feminine Mystique." *National Elementary Principal* 46 (May 1967): 531-5.

    Cites Betty Friedan's view that housewives feel trapped in their family roles and recommends that schools tap into mothers' skills and talents by using them as volunteer nurse's helpers and secretaries--with no sense of irony about the narrow roles he offers in response to the constrictions of domesticity.

63. "How the Profession Feels About Teacher Aides." *NEA Journal* 56 (November 1967): 16-7.

    Reveals results of a survey in which one in five teachers reported having a paid or unpaid aide performing mostly clerical duties. Among the findings: teachers' belief that improving salaries was more important than developing volunteer labor and teachers' concern that the availability of aides would lead to larger classes.

64. Jensen, Pauline L. "In Minneapolis: Hundreds of Volunteers Help Teachers Teach Better." *Grade Teacher* 85 (September 1967): 90-2.

Advocates recruiting housewives, executives, and retirees to give classroom lectures on a variety of topics. The program described was so successful that it received federal funding and required the assistance of additional paid staff.

65. Klebaner, Ruth Perlman. "School Volunteers: A New Challenge." *National Elementary Principal* 46 (May 1967): 13-7.

    Discusses issues involved in using volunteers and suggests that teachers plan and direct volunteers' tasks.

66. Levenson, Dorothy. "Mothers Bring Their Skills to School." *Parents Magazine and Better Homemaking,* February 1967, 48-9.

    Urges women to put their unused skills to work as volunteers.

67. "Pint-Size Tutors Learn by Teaching." *American Education* 3 (April 1967): 20.

    Argues that among California sixth-graders tutoring first-graders, the experience instilled a desire to become teachers in girl tutors and corrected misbehavior among boys who tutored.

68. Provus, Malcolm. *Staffing for Better Schools (Under Title I, Elementary and Secondary Education Act of 1965).* Bethesda, Maryland: ERIC Document Reproduction Service, ED 034717, 1967.

    Asserts that volunteers, because they are irregular and unpaid workers, fail to develop the same close relationships with teachers that paid aides do. Describes various programs, including one enlisting working fathers as positive role models. One chapter covers children tutoring each other.

69. Reed, Betty Jane. "Thank You for Coming! Minneapolis Schools Welcome Volunteers in

Their Community Resource Program." *Instructor* 77 (October 1967): 77-8.

Describes the program's organization and operation and includes two pictures depicting men and three showing women as volunteers.

70. Shapiro, Annette Frank, and Lee Bennnett Hopkins. "Pupil-Teachers." *Reading Teacher* 21 (November 1967): 128-9.

Claims that Harlem sixth-graders can infuse first-graders with a love of reading at weekly story hours.

71. Shipp, Mary E. "Teacher Aides: A Survey." *National Elementary Principal* 46 (May 1967): 30-3.

Recounts extremely useful survey results from two-hundred fifty-one school systems with enrollments over twelve thousand. Describes the "typical" paid vs. unpaid aide, and reports the New York City school system ratio of paid to volunteer aides as 9,150 to 1,850.

72. Stouffer, Russell G., and Patrick Groff. "Should You Use Pupil Tutors?" *Instructor* 77 (August-September 1967): 35.

Advocates use of students as tutors with cautionary advice that teachers supervise closely.

73. Stradley, William E. "Who Was That Stranger I Saw in Your Classroom?" *Grade Teacher* 85 (September 1967): 88-9.

Maintains that teaching-parents can promote public relations by augmenting classroom instruction and field trips and by working with adult groups to discuss solutions to common problems of parenting.

74. Thomas, S. Louise. "'Listening Mothers'." *Instructor* 77 (October 1967): 20-1.

Suggests using volunteers to listen to individual first-graders retell stories from their reading to improve their comprehension and communication.

75. Wolman, Thelma G., and Florence D. Shelley. "Volunteers in the Public School: Bonus or Burden?" *National Elementary Principal* 46 (May 1967): 34-7.

    Posits a growing acceptance of volunteers in the classroom. Focuses on New Rochelle, New York, housewives--some with experience as social workers, nurses, and psychologists--whose unpaid work allows the school district to provide programs beyond what tax resources would allow.

1968

76. Association for Childhood Education International. *Aides to Teachers and Children*. Washington, D.C.: The Association, 1968.

    Asserts that every teacher must have a classroom assistant, paid or not; suggests mothers, sixth-graders, and teenagers as potential volunteers. Photographs of men and women working with children appear throughout.

77. Craymer, Helen S. "'Hart Day': Parents Take Over So Teachers Can Attend a Guidance Conference." *Instructor* 77 (March 1968): 47.

    Mentions that mothers staff classrooms so teachers can meet every two weeks to discuss problem children.

78. Donahue, Mary Marans. "Personality Differences Between Volunteers and Professionals." Ph.D. dissertation, St. John's University, 1968.

    Compares sixty-two women school volunteers with sixty-four teachers and finds the only significant difference (of several factors considered) to be that of age, with teachers younger on the average than volunteers.

79. Eberly, Donald J. "Service Experience and Educational Growth." *Educational Record* 49 (Spring 1968): 197-205.

Advocates granting college credit to students involved in community service activities and describes the approach at Harvard, Radcliffe, California State College at Los Angeles, and Franconia College in New Hampshire as well as a regional effort among forty-seven southern institutions of higher education.

80. Gross, Melvyn. "Teacher's 'Big' Helper." *School Activities* 39 (March 1968): 20-1.

Promotes the use of high-school students in the Future Teachers of America club for individualized tutoring of elementary students; five photographs depict only young women in the role of volunteer.

81. Harre, David. "The Alley Library." *Top of the News* 24 (January 1968): 208-11.

Describes a Washington, D.C., neighborhood library and after-school program staffed mostly by volunteers, including one from VISTA.

82. Iacolucci, Grace M. "Parents as Teachers Aides." *Childhood Education* 44 (March 1968): 424-7.

A series of fourteen pictures and captions emphasizing the rewards of volunteer work; four photos depict men in volunteer roles.

83. Janowitz, Gayle. *After School Study Centers: Experimental Materials and Clinical Research. Final Report.* Bethesda, Maryland: ERIC Document Reproduction Service, ED 051342, 1968.

Describes four after-school tutoring programs for disadvantaged children in Chicago; based on the author's role as principal investigator during a three-year study of the four programs, sponsored by the U.S. Office of Education.

84. Jordan, William C. "How to Put Parents to Work in the Classroom." *Nation's Schools* 81 (February 1968): 76-7.

Describes volunteer work, including fathers' explanations of their paid jobs, at thirteen San Raphael, California, schools.

85. LeBoeuf, Flores. "Qui Docet Discit--He Who Teaches, Learns." *Science Teacher* 35 (January 1968): 53-6.

Asserts that suburban Massachusetts students teaching science and math to younger inner-city students can overcome their own racism and sexism.

86. Los Angeles City Schools. Office of Urban Affairs. *How to Organize a School Volunteer Program in Individual Schools and Suggested Volunteer Aids.* Bethesda, Maryland: ERIC Document Reproduction Service, ED 036463, 1968.

Addresses principals and teachers regarding recruiting and selection of volunteers and outlines teachers' responsibilities. Includes a form letter from children and faculty expressing appreciation for volunteers.

87. Moon, Eric. "Manpower: A Soviet Solution?" *Library Journal* 93 (February 1, 1968): 493.

Advocates emulation of Soviet libraries' reliance on reader-volunteers for staffing; asserts that use of more volunteers in U.S. libraries would foster higher materials budgets and greater service to patrons.

88. Motzkus, John E. "Compliments of the Service Gents." *Today's Education* 57 (September 1968): 14-6.

Suggests solving the problem of teenagers' underachievement and delinquency in Anaheim, California, by involving problem boys in Kiwanis Club-sponsored service projects.

89. Nielsen, Wilhemine R. "Parents Enrich Classroom Program." *Childhood Education* 44 (March 1968): 416-9.

Describes weekly meetings of mothers and grandmothers to prepare instructional materials; suggests using volunteers to handle clerical duties and staff school libraries and fathers to demonstrate equipment they use on the job.

90. Regional Conference for College Social Service Organizations. Cornell University. February 9-11, 1968. *Beyond the Ivory Tower: Social Responsibility and the College Student*. Ithaca, New York: The Conference, 1968.

Compiles conference papers expressing a variety of theoretical, philosophical, and practical concerns including volunteers' motives and the interaction between volunteer and "voluntee." Includes a speech by Dr. Kenneth Clark exploring tensions between blacks and whites and how they shape volunteer work.

91. Rime, Laura, and Jane Ham. "Sixth-Grade Tutors." *Instructor* 77 (March 1968): 104-5.

Outlines the use of sixth-grade boys with low reading skills to tutor second-graders, claiming that both groups' reading improved as a result.

92. Skjoiten, Mae, and Robert M. Bartlett. "Student Volunteers as Group Leaders in Elementary Schools." *Children* 15 (November-December 1968): 225-8.

Reports on the use of junior-college volunteers in Minnesota to help small groups of same-age, same-sex elementary students adjust to school demands.

93. Stone, Virginia. "Interest Stimulators." *Instructor* 77 (March 1968): 99.

Justifies the use of volunteers at an Alamo Heights school by pointing out that the school did not qualify for federal funds and had only limited budgetary resources.

94. "TEAM Volunteers Cut School Failures." *Aging*, May 1968, pp. 6-8.

Promotes the participation of people over forty in tutoring disadvantaged students. Of seven accompanying photographs, one shows a male volunteer.

95. Troutner, Joan, and Norma Musar. "Parent Aides for Public Kindergarten...A Pilot Project." *Arizona Teacher* 56 (May 1968): 16-8.

Recommends incorporating volunteers into educational programs when enrollment increases outdistance budgets allotted for teachers' and aides' salaries. Includes five photographs of mother-volunteers at schools in Tucson, Arizona.

96. "Winnetka 'Idea' Reaches Out." *Aging*, July 1968, pp. 6-7.

Reports on activities at an Administration on Aging-sponsored seminar for school administrators, volunteer directors, and aging-agency representatives. Both pictures depict men as volunteers.

97. Wolf, Elinor. "Reveille for Volunteers." *American Education* 4 (November 1968): 26-8.

Cites the growth of volunteer services in New York, Boston, and Detroit and warns that training must accompany enthusiasm for volunteers to be effective workers.

1969

98. Bahr, Jerome. "Non-Professional Teachers Enliven the Subject Matter." *Clearing House* 43 (April 1969): 494-6.

Summarizes interviews with forty-five volunteers involved in a U.S. Office of Education pilot project in which they visit Washington, D.C. schools to talk about their government and industry jobs.

99. Fleming, J. Carl. "Pupil Tutors and Tutees Learn Together." *Today's Education* 58 (October 1969): 22-4.

Reports that every upper-grade student in the Portland, Oregon, schools system must prepare lessons and tutor a younger student, for the benefit of all students.

100. Fuentes, Martha A. "Reading, Writing, Rithmetic--and Love." *School Activities* 40 (1969): 4-5.

Notes that students and faculty wives from the University of South Florida tutor mainly black youngsters. A white female college student tutoring three black boys is shown in a photograph.

101. Lippitt, Peggy. "Children Can Teach Other Children." *Instructor* 78 (May 1969): 41.

Advocates "Cross-Age Helping" as beneficial to older and younger students but warns that teachers' positive attitude and participation are keys to the program's success.

102. Massachusetts Council for Public Schools, Inc. Project for Adult Literacy. "Teaching Adults to Read: Research and Demonstration in a Program of Volunteer Community Action."

Bethesda, Maryland: ERIC Document
Reproduction Service, ED 039417, 1969.

Presents statistical data on students and volunteer tutors, including more than one-hundred tables and figures. Shows the ratio of women to men volunteer tutors to be four to one and of women to men students to be one to three.

103. Melaragno, Ralph J., and Gerald Newmark. "A Tutorial Community Works Toward Specific Objectives in an Elementary School." *Educational Horizons* 48 (Winter 1969-70): 33-7.

Describes the development of a seven-year program in Los Angeles to create a learning community where predominately black and Mexican-American students and community volunteers work together to foster literacy.

104. Rauch, Sidney J., ed. *Handbook for the Volunteer Tutor*. Newark: International Reading Association, 1969. (Also available as ED 094311.)

Covers such topics as the tutor-student relationship, basic teaching methods, and materials, with contributions from various authors.

105. Robb, Mel H. *Teacher Assistants: A Blueprint for a Successful Volunteer-Aide Program*. Columbus, Ohio: Charles E. Merrill Publishing Co., 1969.

A thorough overview of the benefits and potential problems inherent in unpaid labor. Reports that fifty-one percent of teachers surveyed by the National Education Association preferred not to have aides in their classrooms. Enumerates page after page of tasks volunteers are capable of performing.

106. Steeger, Henry. *You Can Remake America.*
Garden City, New York: Doubleday & Company,
Inc., 1969.

Asserts that blacks should work as volunteers in libraries, schools, literacy programs, and other community organizations to further the cause of civil rights.

107. Thelen, Herbert A. "Tutoring by Students."
School Review 77 (September-December 1969):
229-44.

Argues that student tutoring helps the tutors as much as the tutees and can eradicate racial and socioeconomic prejudice.

108. "They Can't Say No." *Adult Education* 5 (May 1969): 28.

Posits that people will volunteer when approached and cites as evidence the school volunteer work of seventy-five suburban housewives and three-hundred women from a predominately black neighborhood in Newark, New Jersey. Charts growth of the program to more than one thousand volunteers, including a young men's group helping police maintain order at evening events.

109. U.S. Department of Labor. Manpower Administration. *Americans Volunteer.*
Manpower/Automation Research Monograph No. 10, Washington, D.C.: Government Printing Office, 1969.

Reports the results of the first nationwide survey of volunteers with indications that more women than men volunteer and that most women volunteers serve in hospitals, education, and social service.

110. Weed, Florence C. "When a Student Needs a Friend Is When Teachers in Winnetka, Illinois, Turn to Their Pool of School Volunteers." *Grade Teacher* 86 (March 1969): 30.

Emphasizes male volunteers helping troubled boys.

111. "Where Student Activists are VIP's." *American Education* 5 (August-September 1969): 27.

Supports the idea that college students who volunteer should receive university grants for transportation and administrative costs; describes a University of Illinois program coordinating nine-hundred students gaining vocational training by volunteering in education, social work, and nursing.

112. Wright, Betty Atwell. *Teacher Aides to the Rescue: Program Guidelines for Better Home-School-Community Partnerships.* New York: The John Day Co., 1969.

Includes a chapter called "When Parents Teach Too" specifically devoted to the issue of volunteers who enrich the curriculum by giving vocational lectures. The remainder of the book is useful for understanding the role of aides in general.

1970

113. Allen, James E. *The Right to Read: The Role of the Volunteer.* Bethesda, Maryland: ERIC Document Reproduction Service, ED 039113, 1970.

Claims that illiteracy is such a massive and complicated problem that it requires non-professional and private resources from outside the educational system to conquer; also argues the need to overcome the system's resistance to such help from outsiders.

114. Bernstein, Margery R. "Volunteers to Help Individuals." *Instructor* 80 (August-September 1970): 36-7.

Traces development of Mamaroneck, New York, public-school volunteers who assisted in the library and lunchroom and eventually expanded duties to include providing one-to-one attention to students when neither teachers nor paid aides could.

115. Brighton, Howard. "Thoughts on the Teacher Aide Program." *Adult Leadership* 19 (October 1970): 117-9.

   Generalizes that paid aides are more dependable than volunteers; mentions mothers' and fathers' roles as volunteers and suggests that men serve as a valuable sex-role model.

116. Burrow, Daniel Alfred. "Summer Tutoring: An Investigation of Older Volunteer Students Tutoring Younger Students in Arithmetic Computation." Ed.D. dissertation, University of Maryland, 1970.

   Finds that tutees but not tutors improved their math skills as a result of tutoring, suggesting that older students should not be taken out of the classroom to tutor younger students unless compensated. Recommends that teachers who want to see the fastest, most significant improvements should begin with girl tutors because tutees learn more from female tutors.

117. Caplin, Morris D. "An Invaluable Resource: The School Volunteer." *Clearing House* 45 (September 1970): 10-4.

   Covers volunteer services in San Francisco, Philadelphia, Boston, and elsewhere, and notes that the volunteer movement began with housewives and students but expanded to include businessmen and retirees.

118. Cohen, Royce. "Partners for Literacy." *American Education* 6 (June 1970): 36.

   Describes the work of Literacy Volunteers, Inc., founded in 1967 in Syracuse, New York;

emphasizes the training workshops volunteers attend before being allowed to tutor adults.

119. Community Services Planning Council. *The Neighborhood Study Center Teacher Aide Program: 1969-1970 Evaluation*. Bethesda, Maryland: ERIC Document Reproduction Service, ED 060164, 1970.

Reports responses to questionnaires returned by tutors, students, teachers, and teacher aides regarding the effectiveness of after-school study centers staffed by volunteers in Sacramento, California. Includes a guide for supervisors.

120. Community Services Planning Council. *Tutoring Techniques for Use in Neighborhood Study Centers. Neighborhood Study Center and Teacher Aide Program: Volunteer Guide*. Bethesda, Maryland: ERIC Document Reproduction Service, ED 060165, 1970.

Suggests learning activities for elementary-school children and advises on tutor behavior.

121. Erb, Jane. "Springfield School Volunteers." *School and Community* 56 (February 1970): 14-5.

Outlines the activities of volunteers giving the equivalent of 1,094 eight-hour days of unpaid work in thirty-eight schools.

122. Gordon, Ira J. *Parent Involvement in Compensatory Education*. Bethesda, Maryland: ERIC Document Reproduction Service, ED 039954, 1970.

Places the blame for disadvantaged students' poor academic achievement on mothers and describes ways to involve mothers in school and learning activities, including as unpaid workers.

123. Harstead, Pat, and Herb Venner. "Project to Utilize Volunteers in Eliminating Adult Illiteracy. Quarterly Progress Report. First

Quarter." Bethesda, Maryland: ERIC Document Reproduction Service, ED 047238, 1970.

Discusses Adult Basic Education efforts of teachers, aides and volunteers instructing Indian- and Mexican-Americans in their homes. Reprints the syllabus for a thirty-hour training session for instructors.

124. Harstead, Pat, and Herb Venner. "Project to Utilize Volunteers in Eliminating Adult Illiteracy. Quarterly Report. Second Quarter." Bethesda, Maryland: ERIC Document Reproduction Service, ED 047239, 1970.

Documents increased enrollments and notes that twenty-three of the thirty-seven volunteers giving in-home, individualized tutoring are certified teachers.

125. Jensen, Mary Dodd, and Ron Hamm. "The School Resources Volunteer Story: Berkeley, California." In *Educational Manpower: From Aides to Diffferentiated Staff Patterns*, pp. 89-102. Edited by James L. Olivero and Edward G. Buffie Bloomington, Indiana: Indiana University Press, 1970.

Advocates use of volunteers to alleviate staff shortages wrought by taxpayers' refusal to support public schools adequately. Describes a program with one hundred fifty volunteers in 1962 growing to six hundred fifty by 1965. Three photographs show two female volunteers working with boys and girls and one male working with a boy.

126. Keltz, Dave, and Bill Milligan. "Project to Utilize Volunteers in Eliminating Adult Illiteracy: Butte, Montana." Bethesda, Maryland: ERIC Document Reproduction Service, ED 047237, 1970.

Describes teams of teachers, teacher aides, and volunteers dispatched to illiterate adults' homes to provide reading instruction as part of the Adult Basic Education program.

127. Koretsky, Edna. "The School Volunteer Project in Boston." In *Educational Manpower: From Aides to Differentiated Staff Patterns,* pp. 103-27. Edited by James L. Olivero and Edward G. Buffie. Bloomington, Indiana: Indiana University Press, 1970.

Maintains that volunteers' first priority should be production of a "better educated" child, relegating civil rights, poverty, and school-community relations issues to secondary status. Also claims, though, that volunteer programs can help break down racist and classist stereotypes. Argues against volunteer programs run by school districts (preferring private organizations or associations) because they tend to perpetuate outmoded, counter-productive educational philosophy.

128. Laubach, Frank C., and Robert S. Laubach. "Role of the Volunteer Teacher." *Harvard Educational Review* 40 (1970): 277-9.

Claims that empathy and the ability to be the student's friend are important to the "each one teach one" philosophy. Suggests the massive numbers of volunteers needed can be recruited through labor unions, Boy Scouts, women's groups and the like.

129. Parten, Carroll B. "A Training Program for Volunteers." *Young Children* 26 (October 1970): 27-33.

Describes a six-week training project for predominately Mexican-American women interested in working with a Los Angeles Head Start program. Includes stereotypes about Latinas and carries the underlying message that Head Start programs can train women to be better mothers.

130. "Proceedings of the Right to Read: The Role of the Volunteer." Bethesda, Maryland: ERIC

Document Reproduction Service, ED 045317, 1970.

Recounts debates of volunteer issues by participants in the Right to Read Workshop sponsored by the U. S. Office of Education and the Washington Technical Institute in March of 1970.

131. Schoeller, Arthur W., and David A. Pearson. "Better Reading Through Volunteer Reading Tutors." *The Reading Teacher* 23 (April 1970): 225-30.

Reports on a Milwaukee tutoring program using the Spache Diagnostic Reading Scales as a pre- and post-test of one-hundred fifteen predominately black children to indicate that their reading and their attitudes toward reading improved after three months of meetings with volunteer tutors.

132. Sekowsky, Jo Anne. "Parents as Listeners." *Instructor* 80 (August-September 1970): 137.

Recommends using mothers as volunteers to listen to individual slow readers read aloud because they have more patience than do teachers who spend the whole day in the classroom.

133. Sindledecker, Charles. "Volunteer Mothers Ease Teacher's Task." *Educational Screen and Audiovisual Guide* 49 (January 1970): 10.

Advises that teachers can be freed to give individualized instruction when mothers facilitate group learning by volunteering to handle media.

134. Smith, Mildred B. "To Educate Children Effectively We Must Involve Parents." *Instructor* 80 (August/September 1970): 119-21.

Advises parents to help their children by becoming involved in the schools through attendance at parent-teacher meetings and through school volunteer work.

Promotion of Literacy 31

135. Staley, Gerald J. "Volunteer Aides in Public Schools: Policies and Procedures in Oregon and Washington." Bethesda, Maryland: ERIC Document Reproduction Service, ED 041862, 1970.

Collects guidelines, procedures, helpful hints, and forms; published in response to a survey of schools in Washington and Oregon which indicated that little thought was given to legal and professional ramifications of using volunteer aides.

136. Swanson, Mary T. "Your Volunteer Program: Organization and Administration of Volunteer Programs." Bethesda, Maryland: ERIC Document Reproduction Service, ED 052414, 1970.

Claims that volunteers at all levels of the educational system can help solve the problem evoked by the phrase "Why Johnny Can't Read." Supports the notion that women with grown children need a fulfilling activity such as volunteer work.

137. Talbot, Virginia. "Teacher Aides." *Grade Teacher* 88 (November 1970): 109-11.

Suggests teachers look over students' files at the beginning of the school year to pinpoint potential volunteer mothers and then recruit those thus chosen when they take their children to school.

138. U.S. Department of Health, Education, and Welfare. Office of Citizen Participation. *Volunteers in Education: Materials for Volunteer Programs and the Volunteer.* Washington, D.C.: Government Printing Office, 1970.

Compiles and reprints materials on the training and utilization of volunteer workers in schools in Los Angeles, Philadelphia, Boston, Cleveland, and Detroit.

1971

139. "The Administrator's Workshop: Volunteer On-the-Job Training Pays Off." *National Elementary Principal* 50 (January 1971): 55-6. (Reprinted from October 1970 issue of *Learning*, the School-Community newsletter of the Montgomery County Public Schools, Maryland.)

Promotes mother-volunteers to tutor children with reading disabilities; advocates paid staff to coordinate and manage volunteer programs.

140. American Library Association. "Guidelines for Using Volunteers in Libraries." *American Libraries* 2 (April 1971): 407-8.

Notes that volunteers may ultimately seek formal education and paid employment in the library science field; provides seventeen guidelines for success with volunteers.

141. "Community-Run Library Attempts to Raise Funds." *Library Journal* 96 (April 15, 1971): 1416.

Reports on the existence of a volunteer-run, inner-city library resisting takeover by the Chicago Public Library.

142. Criscuolo, Nicholas Paul. "Training Tutors Effectively." *Reading Teacher* 25 (November 1971): 157-9.

Maintains that preparation, including "sensitivity training" must precede tutoring. Mentions that the Junior League paid a coordinator to recruit volunteer workers for the New Haven, Connecticut, public schools.

143. Dade County (Florida) Public Schools. Department of Staff Development. *Assisting in the Classroom. An Individualized Volunteer Education Module.* Bethesda,

Maryland: ERIC Document Reproduction Service, ED 081773, 1971.

Focuses on twelve specific duties of classroom volunteers; for use with the Volunteer Handbook (see Item 146.)

144. Dade County (Florida) Public Schools. Department of Staff Development. *Becoming a School Volunteer. An Individualized Volunteer Education Module.* Bethesda, Maryland: ERIC Document Reproduction Service, ED 081776, 1971.

Presents a training package in four parts: motivation, skills, planning for volunteer work, and finding help when questions arise.

145. Dade County (Florida) Public Schools. Department of Staff Development. *Building One to One Relationships. An Individualized Volunteer Education Module.* Bethesda, Maryland: ERIC Document Reproduction Service, ED 081775, 1971.

Includes a series of provocative statements about volunteers for readers' responses, as preparation for on-the-job conflicts.

146. Dade County (Florida) Public Schools. Department of Staff Development. *A Handbook for Volunteers.* Bethesda, Maryland: ERIC Document Reproduction Service, ED 081779, 1971.

Explains that the School Volunteer Program was funded initially under the Emergency School Assistance Program to encourage desegregation. Differentiates between regular volunteers who give at least two hours a week and resource volunteers listed in a directory for specific presentations on request. Includes detailed job descriptions for regular volunteers.

147. Dade County (Florida) Public Schools. Department of Staff Development. *Helping*

Students Develop Appropriate Behavior. An Individualized Volunteer Education Module. Bethesda, Maryland: ERIC Document Reproduction Service, ED 081774, 1971.

Instructs in the use of positive reinforcement to reward students who conform to classroom rules.

148. Dade County (Florida) Public Schools. Department of Staff Development. *Tutoring in Reading and Mathematics. An Individualized Volunteer Education Module.* Bethesda, Maryland: ERIC Document Reproduction Service, ED 081778, 1971.

Emphasizes the human interaction and interpersonal skills of the tutor.

149. Dade County (Florida) Public Schools. Department of Staff Development. *Using the Services of a School Volunteer. An Individualized Volunteer Education Module.* Bethesda, Maryland: ERIC Document Reproduction Service, ED 081777, 1971.

Addresses teachers with a set of hypothetical situations involving problem volunteers; reproduces a form for teachers to use when evaluating a volunteer's performance.

150. Des Moines Area Community College. Project Motivate. *Volunteers in Education. Regional VIII Workshop. Summary Report.* Bethesda, Maryland: ERIC Document Reproduction Service, ED 067365, 1971.

Compiles the agenda of and papers presented at a three-day workshop for academic workers using volunteers. Serves as an excellent overview of nationwide concerns and approaches.

151. Des Moines Area Community College. Project Motivate. *Volunteers in Education. Regional IX Workshop. Summary Report.* Bethesda,

Maryland: ERIC Document Reproduction Service, ED 067366, 1971.

Includes additional speakers and should be consulted in conjunction with Item 150, above.

152. Falik, Louis H., and Sandra Wexler. "The Tutorial Program: What Kind of Answer to the Problem of Academic Deficiency in the Urban Minority Group Community." *Urban Education* 5 (January 1971): 357-77.

Evaluates San Francisco's Bridging-the-Gap program and finds that tutors, even without formal training or appropriate materials, have a positive effect on tutees' performance becasue they provide attention that improves childrens' self-concepts.

153. Gartner, Alan; Mary Conway Kohler; and Frank Riessman. *Children Teach Children: Learning by Teaching.* New York: Harper & Row, 1971.

Asserts that using older students to tutor younger helps both groups learn.

154. Heathman, James E. "The Volunteer--An Educational Resource." (Discussion paper prepared for Public Schools for Cooperative Research (PSCR) Superintendent's Conference, University of Tennessee, April 5-7, 1971.) Bethesda, Maryland: ERIC Document Reproduction Service, ED 048981, 1971.

Declares that "non-working" [sic] mothers, college students, and old people can volunteer as teacher aides and serve as positive role models for impoverished students.

155. Janowitz, Gayle. "Educational Roles for Volunteer Youth." *Teachers College Record* 73 (September 1971): 81-90.

Maintains that attention from volunteers outside the school system improves disadvantaged children's schoolwork and confidence. Contrasts the approach of volunteers with that of more authoritarian trained teachers.

156. Keegan, Francis W., and MacLean, Jean Ann. "Elementary School Volunteers." *Today's Education* 60 (October 1971): 55.

    Cites advantages for schools and volunteers when senior citizens are recruited. Notes that in a Massachusetts program, the volunteers are recognized at a dinner in their honor where teachers wait tables.

157. Leedom, JoAnne. "Linking Up through LINKS." *American Education* 7 (August 1971): 31-2.

    Describes how North Kingstown, Rhode Island, program adds two-hundred eighty part-time volunteers to the school staff on an annual budget of one thousand dollars. An accompanying photograph depicts a young man helping a student with a building project.

158. Lockhart, John. *Guide for Volunteers in Mathematics.* Bethesda, Maryland: ERIC Document Reproduction Service, ED065339, 1971.

    Includes sample referral and progress sheets for facilitating communication between elementary teachers and volunteers in the Oklahoma City school system.

159. Lund, Arline. "Reading: Teaching Migrant Children." *Today's Education* 60 (October 1971): 49-51.

    Notes use of volunteer aides who employ Right to Read materials with Mexican-American students in Florida.

160. Montgomery (Alabama) Community Action Agency. *Information for the Volunteer Tutor.* Bethesda, Maryland: ERIC Document Reproduction Service, ED049417, 1971.

Asserts that volunteering is a citizen's responsibility; describes an Adult Basic Education program employing volunteers.

161. Nyren, Karl. "Cooperation/Volunteers." *Library Journal* 96 (October 1, 1971): 3059.

Editorializes that volunteers could "man" libraries, allowing reallocation of funds from salaries to books, equipment, and construction.

162. Orange County (California) Department of Education. "Volunteer Aides Handbook: Media Center." Bethesda, Maryland: ERIC Document Reproduction Service, ED054789, 1971."

Reproduces the National Congress of Parents and Teachers 1958 statement recommending that school libraries established by volunteers receive school board funding quickly; argues that without volunteers, many schools would not have libraries, thus limiting access to necessary materials.

163. Project VOICE. "A Coordinator's 'How to Do' Handbook." Bethesda, Maryland: ERIC Document Reproduction Service, ED067731, 1971.

Maintains that each volunteer program must have a coordinator to ensure its effectiveness; recommends that the coordinator have prior experience as an unpaid worker.

164. Sainer, Janet S., and Mary L. Zander. "SERVE: Older Volunteers in Community Service. A New Role and a New Resource." Bethesda, Maryland: ERIC Document Reproduction Service, ED 058552, 1971.

Describes demonstration projects using older volunteers, such as the Reading Volunteers Program, Head Start, and a plan to restore discarded books before distributing them to poor children. Tables show the levels of participation by age and sex, with overwhelmingly more women volunteers giving more time.

165. Stavros, Denny. *The Evaluation of the School Volunteers Project, 1970-1.* Bethesda, Maryland: ERIC Document Reproduction Service, ED 059331, 1971.

Reports results of a survey of volunteer tutors involved in Elementary and Secondary Education Act Title I programs in Detroit. Includes useful data about volunteers' occupations and how they were recruited.

166. Thompson, Diane D., and Michael F. Tobin. "Unpaid Volunteers Pay Off for Inner-City Schools." *The National Elementary Principal* 51 (October 1971): 60-2.

Maintains that personnel can be added despite a lack of funds by enlisting the unpaid aid of parents, part-time workers, college and high-school students, women's groups, and retirees.

167. Washington Technical Institute. Division of Research and Development. "Volunteers in Education. Fourth Region Workshop Report 1971." Bethesda, Maryland: ERIC Document Reproduction Service, ED 072023, 1970.

Reports on activities and evaluations of a three-day workshop in Atlanta, sponsored by Project VOICE.

168. "Volunteers in Libraries: An Untapped Asset?" *Library Journal* 96 (September 15, 1971): 2717-8.

Summarizes the guidelines produced by the American Library Association's Library Administration Division.

1972

169. ACTION. National Student Volunteer Program. *Student Volunteers: A Manual for Communities.* Bethesda, Maryland: ERIC Document Reproduction Service, ED 064575, 1972.

Cautions against fear of using "radical" or activist college students as volunteers in a variety of settings.

170. ACTION. National Student Volunteer Program. *High School Student Volunteers.* Washington, D.C.: The Program, 1972.

Posits the high school's position as a link between students and their needs and the community and its needs by establishing students as volunteers in local agencies.

171. Board of Education--City of New York, and New York City School Volunteer Program, Inc. "The New York City School Volunteer Program." Bethesda, Maryland: ERIC Document Reproduction Service, ED101306, 1972.

Describes the program, including the evolution from a small group performing routine tasks for teachers to a large number of volunteers tutoring children.

172. Brighton, Howard. *Utilizing Teacher Aides in Differentiated Staffing.* Midland, Michigan: Pendell Publishing, Co., 1972.

Argues that teacher aides must be paid employees, the pay garnering loyalty and conformity to school rules. Yet the author divides aides into eight categories, half of them involving unpaid labor, including "father aides" who provide "an easily identifiable masculine attitude" to counterbalance female teachers.

173. Brighton, Howard. *Handbook for Teacher Aides.* Midland, Michigan: Pendell Publishing Co., 1972.

The version for volunteer and paid aides. See also Item 172.

174. Brookhart, Norma. *Handbook for Volunteer Reading Aides.* Bethesda, Maryland: ERIC

Document Reproduction Service, ED 061498, 1972.

Follows up on ten-hour training courses sponsored by Lutheran Church Women for tutors of adult non-readers. Offers advice for interacting with clients, organizing a literacy council, and publicizing programs.

175. Carter, Barbara, and Gloria Dapper. *School Volunteers: What They Do, How They Do It*. New York: Citation Press, 1972.

    Notes the progression of volunteers from non-teaching tasks to classroom responsibilities as aides, lecturers, and tutors. Emphasizes techniques for assessing a child's interests and skills level and developing an individualized instructional program. Cited often.

176. Chambers, Jewell C., ed. *ABC's ... A Handbook for Educational Volunteers*. Washington, D.C.: Washington Technical Institute, 1972. (Also distributed as ED 085338; also issued under the imprint of the U.S. Office of Education and distributed as ED 061164.)

    Provides basic information for setting up a volunteer program and reprints sample application and evaluation forms and recruitment fliers. Maintains that each volunteer program must have a coordinator to ensure its effectiveness; advocates that the coordinator have previous experience as an unpaid worker.

177. Coskey, Evelyn. "The Role of the Southern Appalachian Public Library in Dealing with Functional Illiteracy." In *Public Library Service to the Adult Illiterate: Proceedings of a Seminar,* pp. 69-104. Edited by Genevieve M. Casey. Detroit: Wayne State University, Office of Urban Library Research, 1972.

    Surveys library efforts to foster literacy, some of which use volunteers, including a Berea

College program involving the unpaid labor of faculty wives.

178. Criscuolo, Nicholas P. "Tutoring Programs: School Volunteers in New Haven." *Reading Improvement* 9 (Fall 1972): 57-8.

Describes a volunteer tutoring program with the director's salary paid by the Junior League.

179. Criscuolo, Nicholas P. *A Tutor's Guidebook for Remedial Reading.* Midland, Michigan: Pendell Publishing Co., 1972.

Makes a distinction between volunteers for outside-the-classroom tutoring of "retarded readers" and the remedial-reading specialist who works alongside the teacher. Includes a description of the policies and procedures of School Volunteers for New Haven, Inc.

180. Dade County (Florida) Public Schools. "School Volunteer Program. Progress Report September 15, 1971-June 15, 1972." Bethesda, Maryland, ERIC Document Reproduction Service, ED078264, 1972.

Documents with demographic data the predominance of housewives in a program with twelve hundred thirty-seven volunteers giving more than forty-eight thousand hours in three school districts.

181. DeCrow, Roger, ed. "National Right to Read Partners." Bethesda, Maryland: ERIC Document Reproduction Service, ED 068812, 1972.

Includes a four-page fact sheet on Laubach's National Affiliation for Literacy Advance, with ten thousand volunteers tutoring twelve thousand adult learners.

182. Feeney, Helen M. "Volunteer and Professional--The Role of Adult Education." In *Priorities in Adult Education*, pp. 83-105.

Edited by David B. Rauch. New York: Macmillan, 1972.

Recognizes the persistence of conflict between paid and unpaid staff and lists "dos and don'ts for volunteers working with professionals." Declares that stereotypes of volunteers will give way as a more diverse group, including blue-collar wives and former professionals, contributes services.

183. Gaulke, Mary F. "Laubach Trained Volunteer Tutor Pilot Project 1971." Bethesda, Maryland: ERIC Document Reproduction Service, ED 097632, 1972.

Reports that fourth-, fifth-, and sixth-grade boys had improved reading scores after being tutored by volunteers.

184. Goldring, Cynthia. "How to Cut Costs by Using Unpaid Volunteers." *The American School Board Journal* 159 (May 1972): 24-5.

Suggests that if a school board will only ask for volunteers, people will gladly give of their time, using as the example forty housewives in a PTA-organized volunteer effort at an elementary school in Evanston, Illinois.

185. Goodman, Helen C. "The Library Volunteer--III: Volunteers in El Paso." *Library Journal* 97 (May 1, 1972): 1675-7.

Describes El Paso Public Library's volunteer program, noting problems with senior citizen and teenage volunteers. One photo shows a Mexican-American man mending books.

186. Griffin, Bobbie L., and A. Ray Blankenship. "Training and Use of Volunteer Recruiters in Adult Basic Education Programs. Alabama III (Huntsville) Module. Final Report." Bethesda, Maryland: ERIC Document Reproduction Service, ED 086893, 1972.

Finds a decrease in the student drop-out rate when trained volunteers recruit students door-to-door in the Appalachian area. An appendix listing the names of adult education volunteers involved in the project shows all to be women.

187. Hickman, Charles W. "Volunteer Help: Resource in Instruction?" *Educational Leadership* 30 (November 1972): 121-4.

Notes volunteer activities in North Carolina; mentions Elementary and Secondary Education Act grant to hire fifty-seven part-time volunteer coordinators, with a resultant softening of teachers' opposition. One photograph shows a man and one shows a woman as volunteers.

188. Hubley, John W. *School Volunteer Programs ... How They Are Organized and Managed.* Worthington, Ohio: School Management Institute, 1972.

Contends that volunteers constitute an integral part of public education, citing examples from Oregon, Texas, Oklahoma, Massachusetts, and elsewhere.

189. Institute for Development of Educational Activities (Dayton, Ohio). "Expanding Volunteers in Teaching and Learning Programs. An I/D/E/A Occasional Paper." Bethesda, Maryland: ERIC Document Reproduction Service, ED 072526, 1972.

Summarizes ideas generated at an IDEA-sponsored seminar. Claims that volunteers are unencumbered by tradition and can encourage students left behind by the majority of the class.

190. Institute for Development of Educational Activities (Dayton, Ohio). "Toward More Effective Involvement of the Community in the School. An Occasional Paper." Bethesda, Maryland: ERIC Document Reproduction Service, ED 072527, 1972.

Discusses the introduction of volunteers into schools as a nonthreatening way for the community to intervene in the educational system.

191. Jackson, Jr., Maxie C. "A Comparative Descriptive Study of Michigan State University Student Volunteers and the Relationship of Their Background and Individual Characteristics to Student Activists and to Non-Student Volunteers." Ph.D. dissertation, Michigan State University, 1972.

Maintains that student volunteers, student activists, and students who do not volunteer show no significant differences in their backgrounds and characteristics.

192. Jenkins, Harold. "The Library Volunteer--II: Volunteers in the Future of Libraries." *Library Journal* 97 (April 15, 1972): 1399-1403.

Urges librarians to overcome reluctance to incorporate unpaid workers into library staffs; stresses planning and preparing for an influx of volunteers.

193. Kozoll, Charles E. *Administrator's Guide to the Use of Volunteer Teachers*. Englewood Cliffs, N.J.: Prentice-Hall, 1972.

Posits that white, middle-aged housewives and businessmen have been over-recruited for volunteer work because housewives have free time and businessmen seek potentially profitable visibility. Recommends that administrators recruit singles and old people and gives tips for supervising unpaid workers.

194. LeVine, Evelyn, and Paul Schmitz. "Volunteers in Education: Interim Evaluation Report July 1, 1971-June 30, 1972." Bethesda, Maryland: ERIC Document Reproduction Service, ED 078265, 1972.

Advocates the use of clearly stated goals, such as quantifiable increases in reading, math, and library skills, to guide volunteer efforts. Suggests administering questionnaires and interviews to evaluate volunteer programs. Notes that Kansas City School District enjoys more than ninety-three thousand hours of service supplied by almost twelve hundred unwaged workers.

195. Malarkey, Didi. "Barriers to Voluntarism." (Letter) *Library Journal* 97 (August 1972): 2507.

Reports resistance of professional librarians to volunteers.

196. Matley, Marcel B. "Harnessing Volunteer Energy in a Community Library." *Wilson Library Bulletin* 46 (May 1972): 828-33.

Dates the use of volunteers at the San Leandro, California, Community Library Center to 1960, when the library moved to a new, larger building but had insufficient funds to staff it adequately. Gives specific examples of individual volunteers, virtually all of them women, and their specific tasks. Accompanying pictures depict male and female unpaid workers.

197. Moore, Roberta J. "Using Community Assets for Better Learning: College Students Can Help." *Instructor* 92 (August-September 1972): 59.

Describes Walla Walla, Washington, schools' use of volunteers for reading and mathematics tutoring.

198. "The National Right to Read Effort." *Journal of Reading* 15 (April 1972): 480-1.

Describes the goals--including encouragement of volunteer tutors--of the Right to Read Office, the National Reading Council, and the National Reading Center.

199. Opportunities Industrialization Centers of
America, Inc. "Task Forces for Planning
ACTION Volunteer Use in Adult Basic
Education: A Mechanism for Promoting
Innovation in ABE. Final Report." Bethesda,
Maryland: ERIC Document Reproduction Service,
ED 101159, 1972.

   Describes conferences investigating use of
volunteers in Ohio, Nebraska, and New Jersey.
Points out that ABE programs reach only two
percent of the targeted audience because of a
shortage of resources. Includes a chart
calculating the market value of volunteered
services, among other conference handouts
reprinted as part of this final report.

200. Panek, Alice. "Volunteer Aides." *Journal of Reading* 15 (April 1972): 523.

   Remarks that mothers meeting three times a
week with students needing extra instruction are
so gratified by their charges' progress that they
ask to be allowed to work with them every day the
next school year.

201. "School and Community--Partners in
Education." *Instructor* 82 (August-September 1972): 53-66.

   Includes seventeen short features advocating
the use of volunteers in schools to lower the
ratio of students to adults. Seven accompanying
photographs show exclusively women as volunteers
and teachers.

202. Warner, Alice Sizer. "The Library Volunteer
--I: Voluntarism and Librarianship." *Library Journal* 97 (April 1, 1972): 1241-5.

   Advocates use of volunteers, argues against
professional resistance, and notes lack of
preparation in library school for managing
volunteers.

1973

203. *The Administrator* 3 (Summer 1973) Entire issue on volunteers in education. Bethesda, Maryland: ERIC Document Reproduction Service, ED 094313, 1973.

Takes the position that volunteers are a permanent feature of education staffing and the wise administrator will understand how to manage them. Argues that the presence of volunteers allows the teacher to do more diagnosis of student problems and to feel more relaxed.

204. "Big Business Comes to the Aid of Recruitment." *Nation's Schools* 91 (June 1973): 50.

Suggests approaching local companies to fund volunteer recruitment efforts and underwrite training materials costs.

205. Dade County (Florida) Public Schools. School Volunteer Program of Miami. "SVP Leader's Handbook." Bethesda, Maryland: ERIC Document Reproduction Service, ED 117256, 1973.

Describes the role and responsibilities of the paid SVP resource person and the unpaid volunteer chairman. Among the duties of the volunteer chairman is to recognize the potential and develop the talents of the "young lady" who volunteers to perform clerical tasks.

206. Goodman, Leroy V. "Another New Force." *American Education* 9 (June 1973): inside cover.

Editorializes about the importance to education of volunteerism and notes a National School Public Relations Association report putting the number of school volunteers at two million.

207. Hartman, Rose Ann, and Lynn Gatchell. "Volunteers in Public Schools: A Pilot

Project in Georgia." *Kappa Delta Pi Record* 9 (April 1973): 112-4.

Describes VIPS, a Georgia project with pilot funding from the Education Professions Development Act; notes that untrained aides do more harm than good. A picture of a black grandmother tutoring two black girls is included, as is another showing a white woman with a white girl in a school library.

208. Hickey, Howard W. "Recruiting, Training, Utilizing, and Evaluating Volunteers." *Community Education Journal* 3 (July 1973): 33-5.

Emphasizes the benefits of employing volunteers and discusses management issues.

209. Lancaster County, Pennsylvania, Library. *Volunteers in the Lancaster County Library.* The Library, c.1973.

An inhouse manual of policies and guidelines, based on the American Hospital Association's guide, *The Volunteer in the Hospital.* Interprets the role and function of the volunteer staff within the organization and budget of the public library.

210. LeVine, Evelyn, and Paul Schmitz. "Volunteers in Education: Interim Evaluation Report July 1, 1972-June 30, 1973." Bethesda, Maryland: ERIC Document Reproduction Service, ED 095092, 1973.

Follows-up the earlier report (Item 194) with updated statistics, including the fact that fourteen hundred volunteers gave one hundred sixty-three thousand hours of work. Appendices provide breakdowns of various data including male-to-female volunteers in various activities, with a total of one hundred twenty-five men to twelve hundred ninety-eight women.

211. Los Angeles City Unified School District. "Early Childhood Education: How to Organize Volunteers; How and Where to Find Volunteers." Bethesda, Maryland: ERIC Document Reproduction Service, ED 104560, 1973.

Advises on methods for recruiting greater numbers of men, including the warning, "Don't let the female volunteers dominate the few men that you do have!"

212. Los Angeles City Unified School District. Volunteer and Tutorial Programs. "School Volunteers and Early Childhood Education (Community Involvement)." Bethesda, Maryland: ERIC Document Reproduction Service, ED 104563, 1973.

Places parental volunteerism in the context of community involvement in grades K-3.

213. Maerowitz, Inge. "Parents! Bless Them and Keep Them ... In Your Classroom." *The Education Digest* (March 1973): 38-40. (Condensed from the January 1973 issue of *Early Years*, pp. 29-32.)

Argues that a welcoming principal is the key figure in getting parents to work as classroom volunteers.

214. Norton, Michael M. "PR Program Runs Farther, Faster with Volunteer People Power!" *Thrust for Educational Leadership* 3 (October 1973): 22-3.

Maintains that incorporating volunteers into the public relations program can create staunch supporters of the school and enrich resources available to teachers and students.

215. Paramore, B.; B. Plantec; and J. Hospodar. "Project Upswing After Two Years: An Evaluation." Bethesda, Maryland: ERIC

Document Reproduction Service, ED 099820, 1973.

Describes and evaluates the effectiveness of tutoring at demonstration sites in Denver, St. Louis, San Francisco, and Oxford, Mississippi. Notes that the volunteers did not receive training, but that their tutoring was successful because most were women college students majoring in education or homemakers who had worked as teachers or teacher aides.

216. Raim, Joan. "Rolling Out the Welcome Mat to Tutors." *The Reading Teacher* 26 (April 1973): 696-701.

Refers to volunteer tutors by the female pronoun throughout. Recommends training and supervision of tutors to avoid their becoming disenchanted and quitting.

217. Rich, Leslie. "Magic Ingredient of Volunteerism." *American Education* 9 (June 1973): 4-9.

Argues that young people, with adult guidance, can provide important services at no pay, citing Youth Tutoring Youth as one example. One photograph of a black teenager helping a black child; another of a white teen-aged girl with a white child.

218. Smith, Carl B., and Leo C. Fay. *Getting People to Read: Volunteer Programs That Work.* New York: Delacorte Press, 1973.

Provides a litany of statistics documenting illiteracy rates in the United States, then proceeds to a series of anecdotes designed to prove that "One Person Counts." Recommends keying the tutoring techniques to the age of the student and discusses specific ways for volunteers, governmental offices, libraries, local schools, and community groups to share resources and information. The bibliography includes readings for volunteers about volunteerism and the teaching

of reading, lists books for children and young
adults, and provides titles dealing with urban and
race issues.

219. Thurber, John C. *Project VUE: Volunteers
Upholding Education*. Bethesda, Maryland:
ERIC Document Reproduction Service, ED
088192, 1973.

Traces the development of a program enlisting
nine hundred volunteers in the Palm Beach County
(Florida) Schools. Claims that teachers with
volunteer aides became less authoritarian in their
approach to classroom instruction.

220. Tucker, Marjorie P. "Volunteers for the
Library." *California School Libraries* 44
(Winter 1973): 21-2.

Maintains that the federal government
interferes with volunteerism, citing the fact that
Title I of the Elementary and Secondary Education
Act pays the wages of library aides working
alongside unpaid assistants. Asserts that all
parents, even those who work full-time, should
serve as volunteers.

221. Whaley, Nita B. *School Volunteers:
Districts Recruit Aides to Meet Rising Costs,
Student Needs*. Arlington, Virginia: National
School Public Relations Association, 1973.

Discusses the promotion of volunteerism and
the retention of volunteers from a public
relations perspective. Final section describes
volunteer programs in Los Angeles, Denver, Boise,
Idaho, New Hampshire, and Ontario-Montclair,
California.

1974

222. ACTION. National Student Volunteer Program.
*High School Courses with Volunteer
Components*. Washington, D. C.: National
Student Volunteer Program, c. 1974.

Describes twelve programs, most initiated by teachers, for involving high school students in community volunteer work, including tutoring, in order to give them experience outside the classroom.

223. Altshule, Barry. "Adult School in Suburban Los Angeles Fills Community Education Roles." *Community Education Journal* 4 (January-February 1974): 27-29.

Describes adult classes conducted by volunteers in renovated school buses driven to various neighborhoods; among the classes, training sessions for people interested in becoming community volunteers.

224. Baker, Diane Haige. "Effects of Different Volunteer Tutor/Tutee Combinations on the Reading and Mathematics Achievement and Self Concept of Elementary Tutees." Ed.D. dissertation, Florida, The University of Miami, 1974.

Studies the Dade County School Volunteer Program begun in 1972 with Title III funding and by June 1973 using thirty-three hundred school volunteers working mainly as tutors. Multi-ethnic, including Spanish-speaking and Blacks. Presents provocative findings comparing the effects of race, age, and educational background of tutors on Black, Hispanic, and white, male and female tutees.

225. Carter, Barbara, and Gloria Dapper. *Organizing School Volunteer Programs*. New York: Citation Press, 1974.

Addresses administrators with the argument that training, supervision, a well-coordinated program, and an evaluation procedure will overcome opposition to and problems caused by volunteers. Deals with management considerations including examples of budgets of programs from across the nation.

226. Conant, Elizabeth C. "Welcome Volunteers: Parents: An Asset." *Instructor* 84 (August-September 1974): 34.

Asserts that teachers must accept volunteers without reservation to avoid discouraging them.

227. Cory, Christopher T. "Two Generations of Volunteers: Parents." *Learning* 3 (October 1974): 76-9.

States that an established system or program is not necessary before an individual teacher can use volunteers; warns teachers to start slowly, however, because education courses do not prepare them to supervise volunteers. Both of the accompanying pictures show women volunteers. Also see Item 243.

228. DaSilva, Benjamin, and Richard D. Lucas. *Practical School Volunteer and Teacher-Aide Programs.* W. Nyack, New York: Parker Publishing Co., 1974.

Instructs administrators and teachers in the enormous variety of jobs and settings where volunteer aides can work.

229. Greer, E. "Volunteers in the Chapel Hill Public Library." *North Carolina Libraries* 32 (Spring 1974): 25-7.

Traces the pattern of understaffing apparent since the library opened in 1958 and began relying on volunteer workers. Notes the use of retired librarians and faculty wives for professional duties such as cataloging and compiling bibliographies.

230. Helgerson, Linda; Georgiana Bowman; Lois Rubin; and Brenda Smith. "Manual for a Volunteer Services System." Bethesda, Maryland: ERIC Document Reproduction Service, ED 116284, 1974.

Claims that the phenomenal growth of volunteer services means that more than one person is needed to manage/coordinate and that a greater need to rely on managerial methods to control the volunteer operation exists. Part of a series developed with a three-year grant from the Ohio Department of Education, Title III Office, this offers the most striking attempt to rationalize volunteer labor. Replete with systems lingo, there is nothing spontaneous or grassroots about this conceptualization of volunteerism. The appendices are most indicative of the authors' framework, gathering monthly time reports, sign-in sheets, flow charts and the like.

231. Hunter, Madeline, and Sally Breit. "Volunteers in the Classroom." *Instructor* 83 (May 1974): 20.

Declares that teacher and volunteer must be trained to work together and not compete with each other. Recommends using school staff meetings to prepare paid employees for the introduction of unpaid.

232. Industrial and Business Training Bureau. Division of Extension. The University of Texas at Austin. "Establishing Right to Read Programs in Community-Based Adult Learning Centers." Bethesda, Maryland: ERIC Document Reproduction Service, ED 102303, 1974.

Discusses how volunteers can be used in a combined Right to Read and Adult Basic Education project, with outreach programs staffed entirely by volunteers.

233. Jackson, Audrey H.; Diane K. Baker; Nancy B. Cooper; and Louisia B. Wynn. "Plan, Polish, Promote and Practice a School Volunteer Program." Bethesda, Maryland: ERIC Document Reproduction Service, ED 091396, 1974.

Advises on organization, implementation, and evaluation of a volunteer program, based on

practices in the Dade County (Florida) Public
Schools.

234. Lea, William Lowell. "A Model for a
Volunteer Teacher Aide Program." Ph.D.
dissertation, The University of Tulsa, 1974.

Includes a useful literature review tracing a
shift from teacher resistance to acceptance of
volunteer aides. Chapter 4, "A Handbook for
Volunteer Teacher Aides," makes the point that
volunteers will not replace teachers, lower their
salaries, or force them to become subject
specialists.

235. Literacy Volunteers of America. "Volunteer
Adult Basic Reading Tutorial Program: Final
Special Demonstration Project Report."
Bethesda, Maryland: ERIC Document
Reproduction Service, ED 105276, 1974.

Advocates the use of LVA-trained tutors in
Adult Basic Education programs. Describes pilot
projects in New York, Connecticut, and
Massachusetts. Summarizes LVA activities and
reprints an outside consultant's independent
evaluation of LVA, including data showing that the
number of LVA volunteers teaching increased sixty-
nine percent in two years and the number of
students increased fifty-four percent.

236. McGuire, Agnes C. "Volunteers Can Bring the
Help You Need." *School Management* 18
(January 1974): 40-58.

Documents growth of the volunteer labor force
in schools; cites approaches practiced in Los
Angeles, Boston and Greenwich, Connecticut.

237. Moss, Jeanette K. "An 'Open-to-the-World'
School." *Teacher* 91 (May-June 1974): 21-4.

Describes a New York school using paid and
volunteer speakers and program presenters to
enrich the curriculum. Photographs show a total of
four men and two women. A sidebar on Retired

Senior Volunteer Program participants in New York schools accompanies the article.

238. National Commission on Resources for Youth. *New Roles for Youth in the School and the Community.* New York: Citation Press, 1974.

   Covers the volunteer work of teenagers in community projects, with one chapter focusing on "Youth as Teacher," including paid and unpaid tutoring experiences.

239. "Need for Volunteers Cited: New Projects Reported." *Library Journal* 99 (September 1, 1974): 2026.

   Notes the continued growth of the volunteer movement in libraries, despite the National Organization for Women critique of service volunteering.

240. "One Volunteer Experiment." *American Libraries* 5 (May 1974): 231-2.

   Warns that volunteers recruited when budgets are tight also create a drain on existing funds. Asserts that volunteers can bring ideas and skills that professionals do not.

241. Ryan, Jamice, ed. "Idea Exchange: Volunteerism." (*Idea Exchange* 5 (Fall 1974): entire issue.) Bethesda, Maryland: ERIC Document Reproduction Service, ED 114185, 1974.

   Includes information about volunteers in Head Start; discusses tax advantages for volunteers; reprints the volunteer's "Bill of Rights."

242. Schmidt, Susan K. *Utilizing Volunteers to Expand Services to Disadvantaged Adults.* Morehead, Kentucky: Appalachian Adult Education Center, Morehead State University, 1974.

Alerts public librarians to the potential problems of incorporating unpaid workers into library operations and suggests solutions.

243. Seney, Heidi. "Two Generations of Volunteers: Grandparents." *Learning* 3 (October 1974): 80-3.

Surveys how older volunteers work in schools; states that their time and patience are crucial assets.

244. Taltavull, Frances Adeline. "An Investigation of the Effect of Volunteer Tutors and Readers on Reading Achievement of Fifth-Grade Pupils in an Inner-City School." Ed.D. dissertation, Temple University, 1974.

Argues that more people, especially retirees, should volunteer in the schools--even though this eight-week-long study of volunteer tutoring in a bilingual elementary school in North Philadelphia demonstrated no improvement in tutees' reading skills. Appendix includes transcript of planning meeting with volunteers.

245. U. S. Department of Health, Education, and Welfare. Office of Education. *Tutoring Resource Handbook for Teachers. A Guide for Teachers Who Are Working with Volunteer Reading Tutors*. Bethesda, Maryland: ERIC Document Reproduction Service, ED 109643, 1974.

States that the teacher is responsible for assigning a particular child to a tutor and for managing volunteers. For Right to Read participants.

246. U. S. Department of Health, Education, and Welfare. Office of Education. *Tutors' Resource Handbook: Assessment Items and Sample Lessons*. Bethesda, Maryland: ERIC Document Reproduction Service, ED 109644, 1974.

Includes sample lessons for volunteer tutors.

247. U.S. Department of Health, Education, and Welfare. Office of Education. *Tutor-Trainers' Resource Handbook: Part A--Reading Directors' Organizational Guidelines; Part B--Tutor-Trainers' Guidelines; Part C--Teacher-Orientation Guidelines.* Bethesda, Maryland: ERIC Document Reproduction Service, ED 109645, 1974.

Describes local Right to Read Task Force functions; emphasizes that professional teachers are in charge of each Right to Read volunteer tutoring effort.

248. "Using Community Resources to Improve the First Grade Experience: Project Upswing. A Summary." Bethesda, Maryland: ERIC Document Reproduction Service, ED099819, 1974.

Claims that rural and poor schools should use volunteers because they are a source of inexpensive labor.

249. "Volunteers." *Library Journal* 99 (November 1, 1974): 2795.

Reports on the use of volunteers in library outreach services.

250. "Volunteers in Libraries: New and Ongoing Programs." *Library Journal* 99 (July 1974): 1752.

Recounts specific libraries' volunteer programs; notes both the National Organization for Women critique of service volunteering and the National Council of Negro Women position countering NOW with the assertion that many services to minorities would not exist without volunteer labor.

251. Warner, Alice Sizer, and Elizabeth Eddison. "Volunteer Participation in the Functioning

of the Howland Circulating Library, Beacon, New York." Bethesda, Maryland: ERIC Document Reproduction Service, ED 104356, 1974.

Recommends to the Library Board of Trustees that volunteer processing teams handle cataloging and other tasks; asserts teams can work as assembly lines in one another's homes so that women with young children can be included as unpaid workers.

252. Warner, Ruth. "A Teacher Who Did." *Learning* 3 (October 1974): 79.

Argues that the individual teacher's use of volunteers in the kindergarten classroom brings a big return with no financial investment.

253. Williams, Polly Franklin. *A Philosophical Approach for Volunteers*. Bethesda, Maryland: ERIC Document Reproduction Service, ED 099818, 1974.

Emphasizes the importance of the relationship between volunteer tutor and tutee in a two-year pilot Project Upswing, for first-graders beginning to develop learning problems.

1975

254. ACTION. *Americans Volunteer--1974*. Washington, D.C.: ACTION, 1975. (Also distributed as ED 120391.)

Purports to be the sequel to the Department of Labor survey of volunteer work in 1965 (Item 109), but emphasizes why people did not volunteer so as to understand how better to recruit. Does not systematically analyze data using sex as a variable.

255. Adkins, Patricia G. "Parent Involvement in the Classroom: Boon or Bane." *Journal of Research and Development in Education* 8 (Winter 1975): 2-6.

Argues that mother-volunteers' involvement with classroom teachers may lead to mothers becoming more effective at interacting with their own children at home. A paragraph on father-volunteers restates this notion, but also warns that parents should not be assigned volunteer duties in their own children's classrooms.

256. Barnes, S. A. "Volunteer Aides in the Reading Room." *School and Community* 61 (January 1975): 15.

Focuses on mother-volunteers, some of whom are reluctant because they have no special training. Enumerates duties mothers can perform, such as listening to children read and typing.

257. Bender, L. W. "Volunteer: Key to Community-Based Education." *Community and Junior College Journal* 45 (June 1975): 16-7.

Calls for the systematic incorporation of unpaid workers in community college settings.

258. Cacarillo, Elaine. "Haaren's Miracles." *American Education* 11 (April 1975): 14.

Posits that the success of New York City school volunteers is based on students' realization that someone cares enough to help them without receiving pay as an incentive. One picture shows a white man working with a black boy.

259. Columbus, Ohio, City School District. "Volunteer Services System. Handbook 1: Guidebook to a Volunteer Services System." Bethesda, Maryland: ERIC Document Reproduction Service, ED 116285, 1975.

Provides summaries of the series booklets and recommends the system be adapted for local use.

260. Columbus, Ohio, City School District. "Volunteer Services System. Handbook 2: Organizing a Volunteer Services System."

Bethesda, Maryland: ERIC Document
Reproduction Service, ED 116286, 1975.

Recommends conducting a needs assessment before seeking approval to establish a volunteer program.

261. Columbus, Ohio, City School District. "Volunteer Services System. Handbook 3: Information System for a Volunteer Services System." Bethesda, Maryland: ERIC Document Reproduction Service, ED 116287, 1975.

Links the gathering and analyzing of information to the ability to make good decisions regarding volunteer activities.

262. Columbus, Ohio, City School District. "Volunteer Services System. Handbook 4: Program Operations." Bethesda, Maryland: ERIC Document Reproduction Service, ED 116288, 1975.

Notes that many pamphlets explaining how to establish a volunteer program begin with recruiting instead of discussing the extensive planning and preparation of the organizational structure, policies, and procedures needed before recruitment.

263. Columbus, Ohio, City School District. "Volunteer Services System. Handbook 5: Volunteer Personnel Operations." Bethesda, Maryland: ERIC Document Reproduction Service, ED 116289, 1975.

Centers personnel services in the system as the hub of communication with and record-keeping of volunteers.

264. Columbus, Ohio, City School District. "Volunteer Services System. Handbook 6: School Volunteer Operations." Bethesda, Maryland: ERIC Document Reproduction Service, ED116290, 1975.

Applies previously discussed systems approach to an individual school setting.

265. Erlich, Sheldon. "The VIPs in 'VIP.'" *American Education* 11 (April 1975): 16.

Describes the Los Angeles school volunteer program, with eighteen thousand volunteers, including a library staff with no professional librarians. Makes the argument that unpaid auxiliaries boost teacher morale by giving them non-working lunch breaks.

266. Frazier, Melinda L. "Letters." *Ms.*, June 1975, p. 6.

Evokes the problem of mothers who volunteer to run classrooms during teacher strikes.

267. Gold, Patricia, and Adele M. Taylor. "Of Course, Volunteers." *Reading Teacher* 28 (April 1975): 614-6.

Describes the relationship between local school and county volunteer offices of Prince George's County Schools in Maryland, with the second largest school volunteer program. Recommends holding regular inservice classes to help unify volunteers working in different schools.

268. Goul, Jo. "Boise Likes its School Volunteers." *Today's Education* 64 (November-December 1975): 72-3.

Declares that volunteer programs create interest in and support of the schools.

269. Hartman, Rose Anne H. "Voluntarism in the Volunteer State." *Phi Delta Kappan* 56 (May 1975): 608-9.

Mentions the early recruiting of mostly girls for a Tennessee high school's student volunteer program growing out of the existing adult

Promotion of Literacy 63

volunteer program. Notes a change to an almost even ratio of boys to girls working without pay.

270. Jackson, Audrey. "The Volunteer Way." *American Education* 11 (April 1975): 11-17.

Describes the National School Volunteer Program, using Dade County, Florida, as the model to follow.

271. Kuras, Christine. *Volunteer Assistance in the Library.* Inglewood, California: Inglewood Public Library, 1975. (Also distributed as ED111399.)

Discusses the steps necessary to recruit, supervise, and evaluate unpaid workers. Includes sample posters, news releases, evaluation forms and the like.

272. "Libraries of All Types Depending on Volunteers." *Library Journal* 100 (February 1, 1975): 254.

Cites libraries, including the Newberry, where budget cuts forced reliance on volunteer labor.

273. Literacy Volunteers of America, Inc. "Final Teacher Training (Staff Development) Project Report for Volunteer Adult Basic Reading Tutorial Program." Bethesda, Maryland: ERIC Document Reproduction Service, ED 118867, 1975.

Documents Literacy Volunteers of America training workshops conducted for regional Adult Basic Education directors desiring incorporation of volunteer trainers and tutors into local programs.

274. "Manual for Developing a Senior Citizen Teacher Aide Program." Bethesda, Maryland: ERIC Document Reproduction Service, ED 132139, 1975.

Reports that Oregon schools used a 1971 Elementary and Secondary Education Act, Title III grant to introduce elderly people into classrooms as volunteers. Argues that they have a lifetime of experience to draw on and represent a healthy alternative to Americans' obsession with youth.

275. Massey, Jeanne H., and Jean Davis Myers. "Volunteer Mothers as Tutors in the Classroom." *Journal of Research and Development in Education* 8 (Winter 1975): 54-63.

Traces the grassroots impetus for founding the volunteer program in "middle-class" schools in El Paso, Texas, including the Junior League's involvement. Notes assistance from a "big sister" group, Volunteers in Public Schools (VIPS), in Houston.

276. Mastors, Charlotte. *School Volunteers: Who Needs Them?* Bloomington, Indiana: The Phi Delta Kappa Educational Foundation, 1975.

States the need for state-level support of local efforts to incorporate volunteer work in the schools; describes LINKS, Laymen in North Kingstown (Rhode Island) Schools, and VIRIS, Volunteers in Rhode Island Schools, as examples of local and state programs.

277. Miller, Bette L., and Ann L. Wilmshurst. *Parents and Volunteers in the Classroom: A Handbook for Teachers.* San Francisco: R and E Research Associates, 1975.

Claims that using volunteers in the classroom frees the teacher for individualized instruction. Discusses the incorporation of fathers into volunteer ranks with the warning that men can handle children only in small groups or singly. A chapter on volunteer personality types sketches such characters as "Helpful Hannah" and "Sorry Sam" and another segment advises on familiarizing paid teacher's aides with the use of volunteers.

278. O'Connell, Carol. "Project Reachout" in "The Volunteer Day." *American Education* 11 (April 1975): p. 12.

    Describes an Ohio State Department of Education project to encourage its six hundred seventeen school districts to use volunteers. Advocates seeking federal money to support such efforts. One photograph of a woman volunteer with a girl.

279. Palzer, Doris M. "Parent Power at Pennwood Junior High." *NASSP Bulletin* 59 (September 1975): 102-3.

    Claims that parent volunteers can perform many functions without the school having to spend any of its budget.

280. Recruitment Leadership and Training Institute. *Volunteers in Education: A Handbook for Coordinators of Volunteer Programs*. Philadelphia: The Institute, 1975.

    Updates Chambers, *A Handbook for Educational Volunteers*, 1972 (Item 176). Advises on acquiring funding to begin volunteer programs and serves as a thorough, step-by-step guide for administrators new to managing unpaid workers.

281. Reynolds, Mary I. "A Rationale and Recommendations for Using Retired Citizens as Volunteers in Public Schools." Ed.D. dissertation, Northern Illinois University, May 1975.

    Maintains that school volunteer recruitment should target the twenty million Americans over sixty-five years old, for the benefit of students, retirees, and school systems.

282. Streit, John F. "The Effect of an Instructional Volunteer Program on an Elementary School." Ed.D. dissertation, Wayne State University, 1975.

Studies the effects of an instructional volunteer program at a short-staffed Michigan elementary school in what the author describes as a "rural ghetto" begun after a National Right to Read Committee conference in Saginaw encouraged use of volunteers in the schools. Sees improvements in students' grades and attitudes as the result of interaction with volunteers.

1976

283. Bartley, Bayard. "Potential Building Technique (PBT): A Volunteer Para-Professional for the Classroom." Bethesda, Maryland: ERIC Document Reproduction Service, ED 122173, 1976.

Claims that classroom volunteers exist to make the learning environment more pleasant by giving students positive attention.

284. Brock, Henry C. *Parent Volunteer Programs in Early Childhood Education: A Practical Guide*. Hamden, Connecticut: Linnet Books, 1976. Also Syracuse, New York: Gaylord Bros., 1976.

Extolls the virtues of mothers who involve themselves in the work of classrooms and libraries. Offers guidelines and reprints of forms for planning, implementing, and evaluating the use of volunteers, based on a program at a Selma, California, elementary school.

285. Castellucci, Arthur, ed. "Volunteer Mother Program." Bethesda, Maryland: ERIC Document Reproduction Service, ED 129307, 1976.

Asks "Why pay for the cow when you can get the milk for nothing?" and "Why pay for additional librarians or paraprofessionals when that wonderful milk in the form of the VOLUNTEER is available?" Claims that a woman's mental ability has little to do with being a good school library volunteer. Warns that gossiping about the school and the students may prove to be a problem with mother volunteers.

Promotion of Literacy 67

286. Coleman, Jean E. "Literacy Programs, Library." *ALA Yearbook 1976*. Chicago: American Library Association, 1976.

Summarizes programs, including those engaging the services of volunteer organizers and instructors, sponsored by and/or conducted in libraries. With the 1976 edition of the *Yearbook*, this became a standard section and is included through the 1986 volume.

287. Doyle, James R. "Digging for Human Treasure." *Educational Leadership* 34 (October 1976): 26-30.

Describes the use of "grandpersons" as volunteers in Ann Arbor, Michigan, public schools, with Title III funding from the state Department of Education. Two pictures of male and two of female volunteers included.

288. Eberly, Donald J. "Patterns of Volunteer Service by Young People: 1965 and 1974." Bethesda, Maryland: ERIC Document Reproduction Service, ED126376, 1976.

Announces a small increase in male volunteering; shows the predominance of education services in teenagers' and young adults' volunteer activities.

289. Flanagan, Leo N. "Some Second Thoughts on Survival in the Seventies: Or Two Views of the Volunteer Dilemma." *Catholic Library World* 48 (October 1976): 112-4.

Argues from the administrator's viewpoint that relying on a volunteer workforce undercuts the growth and protection of librarianship as a profession. Argues from the new professional's perspective that volunteering provides good experience before entering the job market. Recommends that administrators avoid actively recruiting volunteers but that new professionals seek out administrators who allow participation in short-term volunteer work for the experience.

290. Gold, Patricia. "Implementing Volunteer Services within a School." Bethesda, Maryland: ERIC Document Reproduction Service, ED 122262, 1976.

Provides an overview and includes a recruitment form which asks if the prospective volunteer would like to work at home or trade babysitting duties with other volunteers.

291. Haendle, Connie. "The Community Link: Libraries and the Literacy Volunteers of America." *Wilson Library Journal* 50 (May 1976): 731-3.

Good synopsis of Literacy Volunteers of America's structure and function, followed by accounts of the organization's activities in conjunction with public libraries.

292. Haendle, Connie. *Organizational Management Handbook*. Syracuse, New York: Literacy Volunteers of America, 1976.

Points out the necessity of maintaining an organizational structure to support volunteers' work; contains useful information regarding the Literacy Volunteers of America system.

293. Helgerson, Linda W. "Volunteer Services System (Third Year Report)." Bethesda, Maryland: ERIC Document Reproduction Service, ED126619, 1976.

Claims that volunteers do not need managing but volunteer organizations do. Places the unpaid staff in the framework of organizational theory.

294. Hendricks, Meg, and Jean Enk. "Lighten Your Load with Volunteers: A Guide for Teachers, Administrators, Parents, and Community Volunteers." Bethesda, Maryland: ERIC

Document Reproduction Service, ED162743, 1976.

Advocates extensive pre-planning; addresses the problem of volunteers with pre-schoolers and ways to provide child care and/or home-based activities. Cautions against volunteers who gossip, are political reformers, or seem overindulgent with their own children.

295. Hooper, Richard. *The Good Friends Volunteer Program Evaluation Report*. Bethesda, Maryland: ERIC Document Reproduction Service, ED 132141, 1976.

Surveys Tennessee principals, teachers, students and volunteers; finds unpaid workers helpful overall but prone to absenteeism. Suggests setting up a pool of substitutes for volunteers who fail to report for duty.

296. Illinois Office of Education. *Because They Care: A Resource Manual for Volunteer Programs*. Bethesda, Maryland: ERIC Document Reproduction Service, ED 130250, 1976.

Covers ten problem areas, including teachers' negative responses to volunteers. Describes activities in Winnetka, Springfield, Galesburg, Decatur, and Rockford, and includes pictures of men and women as volunteers.

297. Kies, Cosette. "And Whom Have I Done What For?" *Catholic Library World* 48 (October 1976): 102-3.

Recommends that academic media centers follow secondary-school media centers' lead in using volunteer labor.

298. "LJ: News." *Library Journal* 101 (February 15, 1976): 568-77.

Includes accounts of California librarians organizing against the use of volunteers and of volunteers staffing Detroit libraries and setting up a feminist bookstore-library.

299. McCauley, Elfrieda. "Volunteers? Yes!" *School Library Journal* 22 (May 1976): 29.

   Provides an excellent overview of media center volunteers, placing them in the context of educational volunteerism. Describes varied activities, including tutoring, undertaken in Greenwich, Connecticut, public schools. All eight accompanying photos depict women as unwaged staff members.

300. "METRO Studies Volunteer Use; Tucson Urges Program." *Library Journal* 101 (July 1975): 1480-1.

   Lists several libraries' fledgling attempts to instigate volunteer programs.

301. Moussa, Linda. "Volunteers Offer Library Services to Shut-Ins." *Catholic Library World* 48 (October 1976): 119-21.

   Describes a Los Angeles Public Library program begun with the help of a local women's club.

302. "Reports on Management of Seven Common Chronic Library Problems as Summarized by Facilitators of Discussion Groups at the Fall 1975 and Spring 1976 Meetings of the Wisconsin Library Association Children's and Young People's Services Section." Bethesda, Maryland: ERIC Document Reproduction Service, ED 129283, 1976.

   Addresses the problems of recruiting and retaining volunteers to help in one-person libraries.

303. San Bruno Park (California) School District. Curricular Services Center. "Handbook for Library Volunteers." Bethesda, Maryland: ERIC

Document Reproduction Service, ED237118, 1976.

Asserts that volunteers are needed to keep school libraries and media centers open every school day. Outlines activities and procedures volunteers follow.

304. Savage, Noel. "News Report 1975." *Library Journal* 101 (February 15, 1976): 579-93.

Notes the growth of libraries' dependence on volunteers, in the context of other news items about recession and retrenchment, union activism, and the women's rights movement.

305. Savage, Noel. "Volunteers in Libraries." *Library Journal* 101 (December 1, 1976): 2431-3.

Summarizes union and feminist opposition to library volunteers as well as pro-volunteer opinions expressed at a conference sponsored by the New York Metropolitan Reference and Research Library Agency (METRO).

306. Sequin, Mary M., and Jane Jarlsberg. "Vintage Volunteers in the Library." *Catholic Library World* 48 (October 1976): 109-111.

Maintains that older people offer particular skills, including oral histories and research expertise in their areas of interest.

307. Stenzel, Anne K., and Helen M. Feeney. *Volunteer Training and Development: A Manual.* New York: The Seabury Press, 1976.

Gives advice to those supervising or expecting to supervise volunteers, especially in hospitals, social work, education, and in decision-making positions. In response to the National Organization for Women statement advocating activist volunteering but against service volunteering, argues that the distinction

in practice is not so clear and that women should
be involved in both and especially in decision-
making positions on community agency boards and
committees.

308. Stephan, Sandra. "Assignment: Administrative
Volunteer." *Catholic Library World* 48
(October 1976): 104-8.

Claims that greater use of volunteers in
direct services and in administrative services can
lead to faster decision making and better priority
setting.

309. Trainer, Leslie. "METRO Workshop on
Volunteers in Libraries Sparks Controversy,
Offers Practical Advice." *American Libraries*
7 (December 1976): 666-7.

Reports on the pros and cons of volunteers in
libraries.

310. Winecoff, Larry, and Conrad Powell.
Organizing a Volunteer Program. Midland,
Michigan: Pendell Publishing Co., 1976.

Asserts that citizens who criticize the
schools can be co-opted by becoming volunteers.
Includes step-by-step instructions for planning
and implementing volunteer use throughout the
school.

1977

311. Ainsworth, Ellen. "Parent Involvement in
Schools: A Parent's View." *Thrust for
Educational Leadership* 6 (January 1977): 6-8.

Maintains that the teacher must be an
administrator and that classroom volunteers must
take supervision to reduce the possibility of
hositility between them.

312. Berclay, G. John, ed. *Parent Involvement in
the Schools*. Washington, D.C.: National
Education Association, 1977.

Provides instructions for workshops designed to enlist parental involvement. A two-and-a-half page list of duties parents can perform is heavily weighted toward clerical and classroom-aide activities.

313. Finacom, Arville. "School Volunteers: Vital Resource in a Troubled Time." *Thrust for Educational Leadership* 7 (October 1977): 24-6.

Declares that volunteers traditionally have linked professionals with the community, but with severe budget constraints, they now provide skills and services schools cannot purchase.

314. Gonder, Peggy Odell. *Linking Schools and the Community.* Arlington, Virginia: National School Public Relations Association, 1977.

Builds a strong case for enlisting parents and other volunteers in service and activist roles. A chapter devoted to advice about recruiting, training, and evaluating volunteers ends with a discussion of potential problems, including the opposition of unionized teachers.

315. Hadley, Roy E. "Issues and Legislation Related to Volunteer Utilization in Public Schools." Ph.D. dissertation, Georgia State University, 1977.

Surveys state statutes, court cases, official rulings, state education officers, and other sources to discover the legal status of volunteers, which varies from state to state. Questionnaire respondents disagreed overwhelmingly with the statement that volunteers should receive a small amount of pay.

316. Ham, Wayne. "Effects of a Volunteer Tutor Program on Self-Esteem and Basic Skills Achievement in the Primary Grades of a

Southern Rural School System." Ph.D. dissertation, University of Florida, 1977.

Suggests that volunteer tutoring seems to lead to greater achievement gains in reading among girls compared to boys and among blacks compared to whites, with black boys especially responsive.

317. Hancock, Mary Frank. "Factors Related to Implementation of Programs of Parent Volunteer Classroom Involvement in Selected Elementary Schools of Florida." Ph.D. dissertation, Florida State University, 1977.

Surveys Florida principals, teachers, and volunteers regarding their opinions about school volunteer programs and suggests that all three groups agreed that increased communication between communities and schools was the primary advantage of the programs.

318. "If You Love Me in the Fall, Will You Keep Me 'til Spring?" *Instructor* 87 (October 1977): 74-6.

Stresses the importance of recruitment and training; imparts information about the National School Volunteer Program and volunteer activities in Miami and at Travis Air Force Base in California.

319. Johnson, Simon O.; Barry J. Guinagh; Afesa M. Bell; and Nancy Estroff. "Developing a School Volunteer Program." *Theory Into Practice* 16 (February 1977): 17-22.

Declares simultaneously that volunteers require extensive training and ongoing evaluation but that teachers will not experience increased workloads as a result of incorporating unpaid labor into the classroom.

320. Karant, Vicki I. "Socrates Denied: A Defeat for Community Resource People in the Public Schools." *Phi Delta Kappan* 58 (April 1977): 639-41.

Recounts the attempt to set up an alternative school in Leonia, New Jersey, featuring extensive instruction and lecturing by volunteers, which ultimately failed when the Leonia and the New Jersey Education Associations sued, alleging illegal use of uncertified personnel to teach.

321. Kennison, Pat. "Parent Volunteers: Crucial Helpers." *Thrust for Educational Leadership* 6 (January 1977): 9-11.

Traces the development of parent volunteer programs with the conclusion that classroom volunteers can provide the "parent involvement" mandated by the Early Childhood Education Act.

322. Lyman, Helen Huguenor. *Literacy and the Nation's Libraries*. Chicago: American Library Association, 1977.

Outlines the problem of illiteracy, then focuses on librarians' roles in planning and implementing programs for particular groups. Argues the advantages of using unpaid labor and summarizes the American Library Association's guidelines for using volunteers. Four appendices provide how-to advice, financial, organizational, and bibliographic sources, outlines of specific programs, and summaries of surveys and studies of literacy levels.

323. O'Connell, Carol Patricia. "Leader Behaviors, Leader Styles, and Management Effectiveness of Elementary Teachers as Related to Paid Teacher Aides and Volunteer Teacher Aides." Ph.D. dissertation, The Ohio State University, 1977.

Suggests that volunteer aides view themselves as subordinates supplementing the educational team's work, whereas paid aides consider themselves teacher's colleagues and part of the team.

324. Palzer, Doris M. "RSVP: A Resource for Volunteers." *NASSP Bulletin* 61 (February 1977): 103-4.

Advocates recruiting volunteers through RSVP, as the Peenwood Junior High School in Bucks County, Pennsylvania, did.

325. Salisbury, Robert H. "Citizen Participation in the Public Schools." Bethesda, Maryland: ERIC Document Reproduction Service, ED 153161, 1977.

Surveys St. Louis public schools and finds that seventy percent of the volunteers are women, of whom one quarter are mothers also working at paid jobs.

326. Scullen, Thomas, and David Curd. "Reading Moms: A Program that Works." *Phi Delta Kappan* 58 (February 1977): 498-9.

Describes Mount Clemens, Michigan, middle school use of volunteers working with students to carry out individualized remedial plans under the direction of a reading teacher.

327. "Troubled Schools Turn to Volunteer Helpers." *U.S. News & World Report,* January 17, 1977, pp. 63-4.

Remarks on the growth of volunteerism despite opposition and the increase in male and elderly volunteers. Accompanying shots depict an elderly white man with a black girl; two black women with some black children; and a white woman with a white girl.

328. "Volunteers in Libraries: Guards, PR, Outreach." *Library Journal* 102 (October 1, 1977): 1996.

Mentions numerous volunteer activities, including a reading-improvement program.

329. "Volunteers in Reading (December 1977 issue of *Reporting on Reading*)." Bethesda, Maryland: ERIC Document Reproduction Service, ED 153202, 1977.

Includes recap of the National Organization for Women position against service volunteering and clarification from a NOW spokeswoman who says that the goal of change-oriented, activist volunteers should be to secure funding of the program they serve within one year.

330. Warner, Alice Sizer, and Elizabeth Bole Eddison. *Volunteers in Libraries*. New York: Library Journal, 1977.

Maintains that volunteers are important because they are voters; provides basic advice to board members, directors, and volunteer coordinators regarding all phases of volunteer management.

331. White, Annadale Rhoads. "A Study of the Effects of Trained vs. Untrained Volunteer Aides in Individualized Reading Instruction in Grade Five." Ed.D., University of Northern Colorado, 1977.

Concludes that trained volunteers working under the direction of a teacher are more effective tutors than are untrained volunteers or teachers without volunteers.

332. Wyckoff, Lorna M. "School Volunteers Face the Issues." *Phi Delta Kappan* 58 (June 1977): 75-6.

Estimates that five million volunteers work in schools. Reviews workshops held at a three-day national conference in New Orleans sponsored by the National School Volunteer Program, including discussion of volunteer roles during teachers' strikes.

1978

333. Beck, Lillie Adelle. "An Investigation of Volunteer and Nonvolunteer Parents Concerning Students' Reading Achievement and Attendance." Ph.D. dissertation, United States International University, 1978.

Argues that the presence of a child's mother in the classroom as a volunteer results in the child's improved performance. Includes results from a questionnaire completed by one-hundred twenty volunteers and nonvolunteers.

334. Clough, Dick B., and Bonnie M. Clough. *Utilizing Teacher Aides in the Classroom.* Springfield, Illinois: Charles C. Thomas, 1978.

Includes a chapter on volunteer aides which points out that the community benefits from the increased flow of information spawned by volunteers' involvement in classes.

335. Fleming, Lily; Daniel Bassill; and Linda Stoker. *Literacy: Meeting the Challenge: The Private Sector Involvement in Literacy Efforts.* Washington, D.C.: Right to Read Program, U.S. Office of Education, Department of Health, Education, and Welfare, c. 1978.

Links volunteer labor to private companies' attempts to ensure the literacy of their employees. These were papers delivered at the May 1978 National Right to Read Conference in Washington, D.C.

336. Haugness, Harriette Ellingson. "Administrative Practices Employed by Principals in Selected School Volunteer Programs." Ph.D. dissertation, University of Southern California, 1978.

Provides a good historical overview of the development of educational volunteerism; documents the role of local school principals in administering volunteer programs.

337. Ilsley, Paul, and Helen M. Feeney. "Voluntarism: An Action Proposal for Adult Educators." *Lifelong Learning* 2 (September 1978): 8-11.

Asserts that because volunteer work is questioned by feminist groups and unions, adult educators must focus not on how the organization benefits from unpaid labor but on how the organization helps its volunteers grow as individuals.

338. National School Volunteer Program. "Guidelines for Involving Older School Volunteers." Bethesda, Maryland: ERIC Document Reproduction Service, ED 226478, 1978.

Claims that older citizens--rather than mothers, businesses, and older students--represent the largest source of volunteers available. Suggests getting two references on each elderly recruit, including one from a physician.

339. Niemi, John A., and Eve M. Stone, eds. "Voluntarism at the Crossroads: A Challenge for Adult Educators." Bethesda, Maryland: ERIC Document Reproduction Service, ED 163173, 1978.

Compiles papers from a two-day conference including Alice Leppert on current practice and on recruiting and Paul Ilsley on training volunteer coordinators. Michael Collins, in "Myths and Fears," argues against the idea of volunteer groups as "clubs for bored housewives" and volunteerism as "contrary to women's rights."

340. Slack, Georgia. "Volunteering is In." *American Education* 14 (April 1978): 6-11.

Maintains that Dade County, Florida, school volunteers constitute a diverse group representing different ethnic origins, ages, and educational backgrounds. Claims that they improve students' test scores through individualized tutoring and other services despite funding cutbacks. Five pictures show two elderly women in a series of activities and two photographs show young boys helping each other.

341. Stanton, Vida C. "Volunteers, Another View: How Do the Volunteers Feel about Their Work?" *Wisconsin Library Bulletin* 74 (September-October 1978): 235-6.

Reports on a survey of fifty-one female volunteers, four of whom also with part-time paid employment, in three school media centers.

1979

342. Allerton Park Institute, 25th, 1979. *Organizing the Library's Support: Donors, Volunteers, Friends.* Urbana-Champaign, Illinois: University of Illinois, Graduate School of Library Science, 1979.

Focuses on Friends of the Library groups, but one chapter on "The Management of Volunteers" provides a general overview of the issues involved in using unpaid workers.

343. Bellassai, Marcia Courtney. *Libraries and Literacy: A Summary Report.* Washington, D.C.: National Commission on Libraries and Information Science, 1979.

Summarizes recommendations garnered during a pre-conference session prior to the White House Conference on Library and Information Services. Mentions volunteers throughout, though briefly, indicating the perception that their labor is an integral component of literacy efforts.

344. Damroth, William G. "Investing in a Talent Bank." *Community and Junior College Journal* 50 (November 1979): 28-32.

Suggests that two-year colleges recruit retired business executives to serve as volunteer guest lecturers, as he did in Fort Myers, Florida.

345. "Grandpersons Wanted Here!" *Instructor* 89 (October 1979): 86-8.

Describes Ann Arbor, Michigan, schools' use of "grandpersons" aged 60 to 87. Two pictures depict white men and one shows a black woman as volunteers.

346. Kornblau, Esther, and Myrna Kruuse. "Teacher: Your Neighborhood is a Wealth of Help." Bethesda, Maryland: ERIC Document Reproduction Service, ED 179506, 1979.

Gives tips on how to organize a volunteer reading teacher program.

347. "Legal Status of Volunteers Clarified in Florida." *Library Journal* 104 (November 1, 1979): 2274.

Contributes to the continuing confusion over whether volunteers should be considered employees for insurance purposes.

348. Leggette, Earl C; John L. Shourts; B. Marie O'Banner; and Leon Howard. "Released Time for Inservice Teachers? Try Volunteers (University Professors)." Bethesda, Maryland: ERIC Document Reproduction Service, ED 171673, 1979.

Argues that using volunteer professors is the best way to supply substitute teachers; one professor claims that her volunteer experience enriched her understanding of college students who had gone through the public school system.

349. Longeway, B. "Commentary: Examining Volunteer Expenses." *American Libraries* 10 (January 1979): 10.

Claims that management time spent on volunteers is as expensive as that spent on paid employees, especially early in the organization of an unpaid labor force.

350. Mulligan, Dorothy, ed. *Effective Involvement of School Volunteers. Partners for the 80's: Handbook for Teachers.* Bethesda, Maryland: ERIC Document Reproduction Service, ED 226427, 1979.

Lists twelve steps teachers can take for effective use of volunteers in the classroom. Includes the National School Volunteer Program/National Education Association statement that volunteers should not continue to staff classrooms when teachers are on strike.

351. "Proposition 13 Spurs Use of Volunteers in Ventura." *Library Journal* 104 (May 1, 1979): 996.

Announces the necessity of using volunteers to keep Ventura, California, libraries open after passage of Proposition 13, which decreased their budget by twenty-two percent.

352. Slater, Marcia. "Volunteers in the Schools: A Gift of Service." Bethesda, Maryland: ERIC Document Reproduction Service, ED 176412, 1979.

Devotes five of thirty-two pages to the problems associated with volunteers, such as lack of dependability, gossiping, and teacher resistance, and how to overcome them.

353. Sleisenger, Lenore, and Joyce Lancaster. *Guidebook for the Volunteer Reading Teacher.* Thorofare, New Jersey: Charles B. Slack, 1979.

Expands on the earlier work (Item 43) to posit a broader interpretation of the volunteer's functions, including tutoring older students and those who are not disadvantaged. Lists and describes nine national organizations as resources for volunteer tutors.

354. "Volunteers Assist Staffers, Run Area Libraries." *Library Journal* 104 (February 1, 1979): 341.

Notes advancing placements of volunteers, even while some California librarians continue to protest the use of unpaid workers.

355. Warmbrod, Catharine P., and Hannah R. Eisner. "Operating a Retirees Volunteer Program in Postsecondary Institutions: A Resource Handbook." Bethesda, Maryland: ERIC Document Reproduction Service, ED 181234, 1979.

Serves as a guide to organizing retirees as volunteers on campus; includes information about forty unpaid workers at two program demonstration sites showing a mix of men and women, all with extensive experience in paid employment.

1980

356. American Association of Community and Junior Colleges. Older Americans Program. *A Place for Everyone: Higher Education and the Older Volunteer.* Bethesda, Maryland: ERIC Document Reproduction Service, ED 184644, 1980.

Includes an introduction by Harriet H. Naylor which asserts that volunteerism gives older people access to learning opportunities and personal growth.

357. Banta, Trudy, and Sandra S. Lawson. "Evaluation of the Lenoir City (Tennessee) Schools Retirement Power in Education Project, 1979-1980." Bethesda, Maryland: ERIC Document Reproduction Service, ED201044, 1980.

Reports on the results of a project using twelve Laubach-method tutors working with fourth- and seventh-graders.

358. Dodson, Kathy. "Help! The Answer Can Be Volunteers." *Idaho Librarian* 32 (July 1980): 112-5.

Asserts that librarians can increase "manpower" despite budget constraints by using volunteers.

359. Hall, Lee E. "Volunteer Tutorial Program: A Guide for Administration." Bethesda, Maryland: ERIC Document Reproduction Service, ED 191878, 1980.

Reproduces handbooks for administrators, coordinators, and volunteer tutors working for South Carolina elementary schools. Includes a cost analysis showing the value of volunteer tutoring services, with the actual cost at $4.44 per student versus the cost had tutors and coordinators received pay at $1,054.54 per student.

360. Hill, Corrine Paxman. "A Comparative Study of Formal Volunteer Programs in Educational Settings." Ph.D. dissertation, University of Utah, 1980.

Compares twenty outstanding school volunteer programs, identifying nine features common to all; traces the involvement of federal and local governments and state-ordered desegregation in the growth of volunteer programs.

361. Kellogg, Larry James. "Development and Implementation of a Multi-Purpose School Volunteer Program in an Adult Education Center (Ed.D. dissertation, Nova University, 1980)." Bethesda, Maryland: ERIC Document Reproduction Service, ED 203052, 1980.

Describes the work of twenty-two volunteers in a Dade County, Florida, adult education center, including tutoring children so their parents could attend classes.

Promotion of Literacy

362. Kozol, Jonathan. "How We Can Win: A Plan to Reach and Teach Twenty-Five Million Illiterate Adults." *Wilson Library Bulletin* 54 (June 1980): 640-4.

Reiterates need for five million volunteers, rather than the two- to three-hundred thousand at work. Suggests that librarians are in a key position to identify and recruit tutors and learners. One drawing shows a male tutor.

363. Kozol, Jonathan. *Prisoners of Silence: Breaking the Bonds of Adult Illiteracy in the United States.* New York: Continuum, 1980.

Regards the teaching of reading to minorities in poverty a revolutionary act because it gives them a way to express themselves. Advocates eradicating illiteracy through the use of youthful volunteers operating out of renovated "Literacy Houses" in poor neighborhoods for college credit.

364. Levine, Ellen. "Volunteerism in Libraries." *Bay State Librarian* 69 (Summer 1980): 11-4.

Argues that librarians should reconsider the use of volunteers because it exploits women and allows taxpayers to believe the library can be staffed without cost.

365. Lovelace, Terry. "'Before' You Begin: Feasibility of Aged Volunteers Tutoring Children in Reading." Bethesda, Maryland: ERIC Document Reproduction Service, ED 217382, 1980.

Argues that even trained tutors can harm children with severe reading disabilities.

366. Lucas, Linda. "Volunteers: Altruists or Prima Donnas?" *Public Libraries* 19 (Fall 1980): 87-9.

Reviews social science literature to address problems library administrators may encounter when seeking volunteer staff members to offset budget shortfalls.

367. Mesa, Pete. "Rationale for Community Volunteers in Schools." Bethesda, Maryland: ERIC Document Reproduction Service, ED 202173, 1980.

Cites the need to provide cultural diversity in classrooms as one reason for recruiting volunteers. Asserts that unpaid labor is a cheap and convenient way for poor women, especially single heads of households, to acquire skills and training for securing paid employment.

368. Sannwald, William W., and Catherine N. Hoffman. "Practicing Librarians: Volunteerism in Ventura County." *Library Journal* 105 (March 15, 1980): 681-2.

Recounts the beginning of volunteer activities in Ventura County, California, libraries as a result of staff cuts after passage of Proposition 13. Notes the refusal of the County Board of Supervisors to allow branch closings and the resulting reliance on volunteers, who in their first year donated an equivalent of $54,260 and lobbied effectively for a higher library budget the next year.

369. "School Volunteer Program: A Two-Year Evaluation Report." Bethesda, Maryland: ERIC Document Reproduction Service, ED 189684, 1980.

Declares that Columbus, Indiana, schools use volunteers to stretch the budget, revealing that the seventeen thousand dollars proposed for the program will yield eighty-nine thousand dollars worth of services.

370. True, Douglas, and Patty Ehda. "Parent Volunteer Handbook: Teachers Need Parents-- Parents Need Teachers--Students Need Both." Bethesda, Maryland: ERIC Document Reproduction Service, ED240170, 1980.

Describes California compensatory education programs using parents as volunteers, in response to the Elementary and Secondary Education Act's mandate regarding parental involvement.

371. Williams, Billie, and E. Joanne Dale. "Volunteer Programs Give Big Payoff." *Thrust for Educational Leadership* 9 (January 1980): 24-6.

Praises the seventeen hundred VIPS (Volunteers in Public Schools) giving sixty-three hundred hours of service to Huntington Beach Union High School District. Asserts that volunteer programs exist to take up the slack caused by shrinking education dollars.

1981

372. Brown, Barbara E. "The Identification of Major Competencies and Attributes Needed by Volunteer Literacy Tutors of Adults and the Development of a Tutor Self-Assessment Inventory." Ph.D. dissertation, Northern Illinois University, 1981.

Develops a list of abilities beginning literacy tutors should have and a self-assessment quiz for tutors. Includes information about Literacy Volunteers of America and the National Affiliation for Literacy Advance. Reveals many of the tensions inherent in the tutor-student relationship.

373. Cone, Richard, and Judith Johnson. "Volunteers in Education." Bethesda, Maryland: ERIC Document Reproduction Service, ED204869, 1981.

Reviews the results of nine studies of volunteers.

374. De Pillis, Susan. "Do-It-Yourself: The Grandpeople Project." *Thrust for Educational Leadership* 11 (November 1981): 30-1.

Describes how professional staff at a Riverside, California, elementary school responded to fiscal cutbacks by tapping retirees for volunteer work. Four pictures portray two men and two women as volunteers.

375. Etlinger, Leonard E., and Earl J. Ogletree. "School Volunteer Program: A Resource for the Schools." Bethesda, Maryland: ERIC Document Reproduction Service, ED 204844, 1981.

Reports a ninety-five percent increase in school expenditures in the 1970s and argues that unpaid workers can help maintain educational quality even during fiscal retrenchment. Claims that 2.3 million volunteers work an average of six hours a day in schools.

376. Grindstaff, Gordon. "Back-up Brigade: Volunteer Tutors Lend a Hand." *Clearing House* 55 (October 1981): 84-5.

Describes supplemental tutoring for disadvantaged students in Chicago; includes references to specific male volunteers.

377. Ilsley, Paul J., and John A. Niemi. *Recruiting and Training Volunteers*. New York: McGraw-Hill, 1981.

Couches recommendations for organizing and administering volunteer services in management theory rhetoric. A textbook approach.

378. LeClair-Marzolf, Marsha. "Fairly Boring Jobs for Young People." *Unabashed Librarian* 38 (1981): 2-5. (Letter reprinted from the February 1981 issue of *Main Entry*.)

Suggests that Boy Scout volunteers in libraries need active, interesting tasks, such as reading stories to children, rather than only boring clerical work.

379. National School Volunteer Program. *School Volunteer Programs: Everything You Need to*

Know to Start or Improve Your Program.
Bethesda, Maryland: ERIC Document
Reproduction Service, ED 226477, 1981.

Asserts that the presence of volunteers in the classrooms transforms teachers into managers. Briefly describes a sampling of school volunteer programs across the country; notes the need to recruit retirees to replace mothers who have entered the paid workforce.

380. Purcell, Elizabeth A., and Terry Lynne Nagle. "Volunteers and Older Students." Bethesda, Maryland: ERIC Document Reproduction Service, ED 226426, 1981.

Stresses that volunteers are not teachers, but can smooth desegregation efforts and help motivate students. Published by the National School Volunteer Program.

381. Parrish, William C. "Volunteers in the Secondary Schools: A Valuable Resource (From *The Practitioner* 7, January 1981)." Bethesda, Maryland: ERIC Document Reproduction Service, ED 199898, 1981.

States that program success depends on having an administrator or teacher, that is, a professional rather than a volunteer, in charge. Describes projects in Virginia, Louisiana, Oklahoma, South Dakota, New York, and Arizona.

382. Smith, Ester Gottlieb. *Libraries in Literacy*. Washington, D.C.: U.S. Department of Education, Office of Libraries and Learning Technologies, 1981.

Reports on the results of surveys and case studies to determine the extent of involvement in literacy programs on the part of public, school, community college, and state libraries. Includes information regarding libraries' reliance on and support of volunteers. The second of two volumes comprises appendices of survey questionnaires, an extensive bibliography, interview schedules, and detailed descriptions of the particular libraries studied.

383. Stahl, Norman A., and William C. Brown. "Help is Out There--Here's How to Find It." *Instructor* 91 (August 1981): 80.

Suggests various avenues to search for volunteers, including parents, older students, and mothers' clubs.

384. Wood, Janice. "Volunteers--Worth Their Weight in Gold." *Instructor* 91 (August 1981): 79.

Asserts that training helps retain valuable volunteers.

1982

385. "ALA and Other Members of Coalition for Literacy Announce $1.7 Million Goal." *American Libraries* 13 (July/August 1982): 481.

Announces the coalition's awareness campaign in cooperation with the Ad Council and states that the coalition's function is to provide assistance with establishing and training volunteer groups.

386. Armstrong, Audrey A., and Sally P. Hunt. *VITAL Guidelines. Tutor Training for an Adult Literacy Program*. Bethesda, Maryland: ERIC Document Reproduction Service, ED 244104, 1982.

Serves as the Monroe County (Indiana) Public Library training manual for Volunteers in Tutoring Adult Learners (VITAL), an affiliate of Literacy Volunteers of America with funding from the Library Services and Construction Act.

387. Bernstein, Martha. "Schools and Volunteers." *Childhood Education* 59 (November-December 1982): 100-1.

Points out that just when school budgets force greater need for volunteers, the traditional unpaid workers--mothers--join the paid workforce. Suggests alternatives such as retirees, fathers, and businesses. Sees the dwindling supply as an economic rather than a feminist issue.

388. Blair, Pat. "Medford Storytelling Guild: or Volunteers, Unlimited." *Emergency Librarian* 10 (November-December 1982): 19-20.

Describes the library activities of the volunteer Guild, including a reading promotion project, story hours, and the development of a storymobile to serve children before the Jackson County, Oregon, schools established kindergartens.

389. Chapman, Alison. "Volunteers are 'In' ... in the New Haven Schools." *Educational Horizons* 60 (Spring 1982): 106-8.

Traces the evolution of the New Haven schools volunteer program since its inception in 1969.

390. "Clearinghouse for Maryland Volunteers." *Library Journal* 107 (September 1, 1982): 1589.

Announces that the Maryland Library Association's Volunteer Services Steering Committee will serve as a data collection and clearing house for volunteer efforts in libraries.

391. Cohen, Neal M. "Volunteerism in Education: Translating Spirit into State Action." *Educational Horizons* 60 (Spring 1982): 101-5.

Asserts that the state legislature should support volunteer work in the schools through funding and by taking a positive philosophical stance.

392. De Pillis, Susan. "Recruit 'Grandpeople' as Volunteer Tutors, and Students Will Reap the Rewards." *American School Board Journal* 169 (July 1982): 28-30.

Recalls that a severe budget cut caused the loss of teacher aides at an elementary school in Riverside, California, where the staff turned to retirees to serve as volunteers. Notes elderly people's reluctance to serve in schools where students pose extreme disciplinary problems. One photograph depicts an older white man working with a black youngster.

393. Detweiler, Mary Jo. "Volunteers in Public Libraries: The Costs and Benefits." *Public Libraries* 21 (Fall 1982): 80-2.

Traces the instigation of library volunteer efforts to the Board of Supervisors in Manassas, Virginia, channeling funds to police and schools in response to population growth. Interprets volunteer programs as a service to women who need an opportunity to do something worthwhile.

394. Graham, Anne M. "Volunteerism and Education." *American Education* 18 (August-September 1982): inside cover.

Argues that individuals, not government, must solve educational problems by volunteering.

395. "LSCA-funded Volunteer Program Catches on in Carroll County." *Library Journal* 107 (March 1, 1982): 500-1.

Reports on the first Maryland volunteer program instigated with Library Services and Construction Act seed money, noting that by the end of the first year volunteers were giving one-hundred fifty hours per week and had enabled the library to start new programs.

396. McKinley, Carey. "Volunteer Efforts Recognized at Laramie County." *Wyoming Library Roundup* 37 (Summer 1982): 50-1.

Points out that volunteers from such organizations as the Boy Scouts and the Altrusa

Club can foster an increase in circulation of adult and children's books.

397. Newman, A. P. "Volunteers Keep an Adult Basic Education Tutoring Program VITAL." *Educational Horizons* 60 (Spring 1982): 109-10.

Describes the Volunteers In Tutoring Adult Learners program in Bloomington, Indiana, begun in 1977 with funds from the Library Services and Construction Act and support from the Monroe County Library.

398. Nyren, Karl. "A Year of Turmoil: Threats to Budgets, Volatile Network and Utility Fortunes, Fast-spreading Automation, and an Acute Concern for Priorities." *Library Journal* 107 (January 15, 1982): 139-50.

Includes in this year-end review a discussion of the trend toward expanding use of volunteers in public and academic libraries along with continued staff opposition in some instances.

399. "People Are Your Most Valuable Resources." *Instructor and Teacher* 92 (August 1982): 42-4.

Maintains that volunteers provide human interaction which students need for improved achievement and self-esteem. Includes tips for using working parents and the elderly as volunteers and a sidebar on "How to Start Your Own Volunteer Program," which refers readers to the National School Volunteer Program for more information. Two pictures depict male and female volunteers.

400. "Providence Library Gets $$ to Establish Volunteer Program." *Library Journal* 107 (June 15, 1982): 1169.

Briefly announces the Rhode Island Foundation's twenty-five thousand dollar grant to start a volunteer program at Providence Public Library.

401. Ridge, Aldema A. "The Force: Middle School Style." *Clearing House* 55 (March 1982): 293-6.

   Describes the Senior Adult Volunteer Program in Howard County, Maryland, started in 1977 as an educational innovation with a Title IV grant.

402. Rothschild, Mary Aickin. "Volunteers and the Freedom Schools: Education for Social Change in Mississippi." *History of Education Quarterly* 22 (Winter 1982): 401-20.

   Traces developments in the 1964 and 1965 Mississippi Freedom Schools taught by northern college students, fifty-four percent of them male and forty-six percent female. Pinpoints a shift from a remedial academic program the first summer to direct political action the next.

403. Taranto, Susanne E. "Organizing Volunteers Statewide: Florida Raises an Army of Able Helpers for the State's Students and Teachers Through an Organized and Efficient Statewide School Volunteer Program." *American Education* 18 (July 1982): 20-23.

   Advocates use of the state's Department of Education to promote, manage, and coordinate the activities of burgeoning school volunteer programs.

404. Tierce, Jerry Wood. "The Role of the Secondary School Volunteer as Perceived by School Volunteer Coordinators." Ph.D. dissertation, Texas A&M University, 1982.

   Reports useful data gleaned from the responses of one hundred two volunteer coordinators; among the findings: about sixteen hundred volunteers per school volunteer program give more than fifty thousand hours of service annually.

405. "Volunteer Use Up in Phoenix." *Library Journal* 107 (October 1, 1982): 1804.

Cites less turnover and longer hours among volunteers as reasons for twenty-three percent increase in unpaid labor.

406. "Volunteers in Arlington County Contribute Hours and Know-how." *Library Journal* 107 (February 1, 1982): 215-6.

Very brief, but notes that volunteers catalog Polish-language materials.

407. "Volunteers in Libraries: Reports From All Over." *Library Journal* 107 (January 1, 1982): 20-1.

Surveys briefly volunteer activities, including note that Janesville, Wisconsin, Public Library places help-wanted ads for unpaid workers.

1983

408. Alloway, Catherine Suyak. "Library and Literacy Education in the '80's." *RQ* (Summer 1983): 349-53.

Traces activities of various libraries and library associations in providing literacy services, including subsidizing volunteer tutoring.

409. Anderson, A.J. "How Do You Manage? Why Not Volunteers?" *Library Journal* 108 (May 1, 1983): 883-4.

Poses a hypothetical situation wherein budget cuts lead to discuss of using volunteers at the reference desk. Mary Jo Detweiler's response, "Volunteers Are One Option," cautions that it takes time to plan and implement a volunteer program and to overcome staff resistance.

410. "Children Computer Volunteers Help
     Janesville, Wisc. Program." *Library Journal*
     108 (October 1, 1983): 1832.

   Briefly records the work of fifth- through
tenth-graders working for free in a computer-
assisted summer reading program.

411. Curry, Anna. "Adult Learner Services at the
     Pratt Library: An Evaluative Treatment."
     Library Trends 31 (Spring 1983): 585-97.

   Documents the shift from paid to volunteer
labor in library literacy efforts as a result of
federal funding cuts. Indicates cutbacks in
tutoring services as well.

412. Deckoff, Marvin J. "The Volunteer: Key to
     Successful Fund Raising." *Independent School*
     43 (October 1983): 34-8.

   Focuses on the role of alumni-volunteers in
raising money for schools by contacting fellow
alumni on behalf of the development office.

413. "Docents at Los Angeles Public: An Elite
     Volunteer Guide Corps." *Library Journal* 108
     (October 15, 1983): 1917.

   Announces volunteer recruitment efforts,
especially for bilingual people.

414. Guthrie, Chuck. "A Guide for Organizing a
     Volunteer Adult Reading Program (VARP)."
     Bethesda, Maryland: ERIC Document
     Reproduction Service, ED 252708, 1983.

   Recommends forming a statewide Literacy
Council to support volunteer tutoring efforts.

415. Hettling, Lillian B. "'Chronicles'--An
     Intergenerational Experience." *Aging*,
     March/April 1983, pp. 26-8.

Makes the point that elderly volunteers can contribute to middle-school social science courses by giving oral history interviews.

416. Hoot, James L. "Older Adult Volunteers." *Day Care and Early Education* 10 (Spring 1983): 16-8.

Advocates the use of retired and elderly volunteers because of their commitment to voting and the likelihood that their contact with the schools will lead to their support of children's programs.

417. Horrell, Sallie. "Bears and Butterflies: The Literacy Volunteers of Gloucester (Virginia). Project POWER, 1982-83." Bethesda, Maryland: ERIC Document Reproduction Service Center, ED 244075, 1983.

Describes the development of a Literacy Volunteers of America chapter to provide tutors in existing Adult Basic Education and English as a Second Language classes.

418. "Hurst, Texas, Volunteers Save Library $165,000." *Library Journal* 108 (October 1, 1983): 1834.

Briefly reports the savings over a three-and-a-half year period resulting from use of unpaid workers coordinated by a volunteer.

419. Janey, Jane, ed. "Effective Utilization of Volunteers in Head Start Programs: A Manual." Bethesda, Maryland: ERIC Document Reproduction Service, ED 260846, 1983.

Discusses legal liability, insurance, and official policies regarding free meals and reimbursement for expenses.

420. Johnson, Vance O'Neal. "A Case Study of an Educational Change Effort: The Organization and Implementation of a Community Volunteer Program at Piedmont Middle School." Ph.D.

dissertation, University of North Carolina, 1983.

Posits the introduction of volunteers as a change to be orchestrated by school administrators to avoid teacher frustration and resistance to innovation.

421. Kagan, Sharon Lynn, and Carol Schraft. "Developing Parent Commitment to Public Education: New Directions for the 1980's." In *For Every School a Community: Expanding Environments for Learning*, pp. 24-38. Edited by Robert L. Sinclair. Boston: Institute for Responsive Education, 1983.

Argues that demographic and family-life changes have made direct parental involvement (such as volunteer work) in the schools an outmoded expectation. Declares that parents' political activism and corporate support are more realistic alternatives.

422. Keller, M. Jean. "The Sharing of Life and Learning--An Intergenerational Program." *Lifelong Learning* 6 (March 1983): 26-7.

Maintains that older volunteers can serve as instructors to "latch-key" teenagers, serving both groups' needs.

423. Lander, Faye. "Aides Acquire Marketable Skills." *School Library Journal* 29 (August 1983): 34.

Argues that high-school students who volunteer to work in the media center have a better chance at paid employment later.

424. "Men Volunteers Tops." *Library Journal* 108 (August 1983): 1420.

One-paragraph announcement that four of five Arlington Heights, Illinois, Public Library volunteers receiving awards were men.

Promotion of Literacy 99

425. Riley, Mary Tom, and Libby Balter Blume. "Volunteer Grandparents in Head Start." Bethesda, Maryland: ERIC Document Reproduction Service, ED 235904, 1983.

Argues that senior citizens have a lifetime of learning and the time to give, benefiting themselves and the students. Eleven photographs show men volunteers; eighteen depict women.

426. "San Diego Volunteers Rate $5 an Hour." *Library Journal* 108 (August 1983): 1420.

Notes that San Diego Library rates volunteers above minimum wage when calculating their value.

427. Schulte, Jean Kendall. "An Examination of Volunteers and Attitudes Toward Education." Ph.D. dissertation, University of Missouri-Columbia, 1983.

Provides a good overview of the history and development of specific school volunteer programs, beginning with the New York effort in 1956.

428. Stone, Marvin. "Three Chances to Help." *U.S. News and World Report* 95 (July 18, 1983): 72.

Editorializes that federal funds should be expended to encourage students to work as volunteer literacy tutors for college credit.

429. "Volunteers at Providence Library Help Staff Handle Rising Demand." *Library Journal* 108 (October 1, 1983): 1832.

Announces continuation of a volunteer program funded by a Rhode Island Foundation grant after volunteers gave thirty-eight hundred hours in the program's first year.

430. Waite, Peter A. "The Role of Volunteers in Adult Literacy Programs." Bethesda, Maryland: ERIC Document Reproduction Service, ED 240294, 1983.

Charges that literacy programs have the responsibility to cooperate with other community agencies for volunteer services and fundraising.

431. Warner, Alice Sizer. *Volunteers in Libraries II.* LJ Special Report No. 24. New York: Library Journal, 1983.

    Builds on the earlier report (Item 330). Based on responses to questionnaires sent to more than twenty-five hundred libraries; reports on libraries volunteer programs; notes growth and says it is because libraries are chronically underfunded. Emphasizes administrative and management issues more than the earlier issue did.

432. Welliver, M. Margaret. "A Handbook for Utilizing Volunteer Tutors in an Adult Basic Education Program." Bethesda, Maryland: ERIC Document Reproduction Service, ED 255747, 1983.

    Describes State College (Pennsylvania) Kiwanis Club's volunteer tutoring in a collaborative program with the State College Area School District.

1984

433. Bell, Terrel H. "Toward a Learning Society." *American Education* 20 (April 1984): 2-3.

    Asserts that the entire nation, not just the educational system, is responsible for making "a full and unambiguous commitment to the promotion of literacy" by, among other things, serving as volunteers.

434. Berdeaux, Jack, and Jill Borden. *The Adult Learner. A Handbook for Volunteer and New Adult Education Teachers.* Bethesda, Maryland: ERIC Document Reproduction Service, ED 253735, 1984.

Encourages volunteer teachers to get to know their students so as to establish a close, one-to-one relationship.

435. Borden, Jill. "Volunteerism in Adult Education: A Guidebook for Increasing the Scope and Quality of Volunteer Programs in Adult Education." Bethesda, Maryland: ERIC Document Reproduction Service, ED 253644, 1984.

Purports to be a "cookbook" with "recipes" for successful deployment of volunteer activities. Notes that sixty-four percent of the volunteers in Maricopa County, Arizona, are women and that only six percent are elderly despite the high percentage of retirees in the Phoenix area. Admires hospitals' ability to organize and maintain volunteer forces.

436. Carvalho, Joseph. "To Complement or Compete? The Role of Volunteers in Public Libraries." *Public Library Quarterly* 5 (Spring 1984): 35-9.

Reviews library literature on volunteer staffing and argues that unpaid workers' roles must be distinctly different from professionals' duties.

437. Clarke, Raymond E. "The Development of a Model Program for the Recruitment, Training, and Utilization of Elderly School Volunteers." Ph.D. dissertation, University of Maryland, 1984.

Reports the success of male and "non-traditional" volunteers and the need for more volunteers in most Maryland school districts. Includes a hundred-page manual for developing a program using senior citizens as volunteers.

438. Daly, John H. "Utilize an Untapped Resource." *Middle School Journal* 15 (May 1984): 10-1.

	Emphasizes the potential of "human resources" and advocates intergenerational programming through the Retired Senior Volunteer Program (RSVP).

439. Davis, Lorri. "Senior Readers in the Elementary Library." *Reading Teacher* 37 (May 1984): 913.

	Outlines the use of volunteers as story-readers in school libraries in Dundee, Illinois.

440. Gray, Sandra T. "How to Create a Successful School/Community Partnership." *Phi Delta Kappan* 65 (February 1984): 405-9.

	Posits a revival of interest in school volunteer programs and surveys existing ones around the country.

441. Greene, Bob. "The ABC's of Courage: At Day's End, One Man Learns That He Can Learn." *Esquire,* August 1984, p. 10.

	Tells the story of an illiterate male plumber who receives tutoring from a female member of Literacy Volunteers of Chicago.

442. Harris, Alberta Farmer, and LaVerne Owens. "Franklin Elementary School Tutorial Enrichment Program in Elementary Education." Bethesda, Maryland: ERIC Document Reproduction Service, ED 250075, 1984.

	Includes a "code of ethics" for volunteers in which they agree to professionalism despite the absence of pay.

443. Koehler, C. Russell. "Classroom Supervision of Volunteers: Handbook for Instructors." Bethesda, Maryland: ERIC Document Reproduction Service, ED 246954, 1984.

	Suggests the instructor become a "classroom manager." Describes the volunteer's tasks and the instructor's supervisory responsibilities.

444. Koehler, C. Russell. "Handbook for Volunteer Coordinators of ABE/ESL Classroom Volunteers." Bethesda, Maryland: ERIC Document Reproduction Service, ED 246953, 1984.

Covers the basics of recruiting, training, and evaluating.

445. Koehler, C. Russell. "Handbook for Volunteers: Adult Education Program." Bethesda, Maryland: ERIC Document Reproduction Service, ED246955, 1984.

Explains the need for volunteers in overcrowded, understaffed, tuition-free courses funded by the Adult Education Act.

446. Lane, Martha A. *Handbook for Volunteer Reading Aides.* Bethesda, Maryland: ERIC Document Reproduction Service, ED 256900, 1984.

Suggests incorporating microcomputers into the teaching of reading and writing skills. Provides a brief history of literacy and the promotion of literacy, especially by Lutheran Church Women. Reprints a student's poem critical of Reaganomics.

447. Mattleman, Marciene S. "Mayor's Commission on Literacy in Philadelphia. Final Narrative/Report." Bethesda, Maryland: ERIC Document Reproduction Service, ED 246263, 1984.

Argues that volunteer tutors must be integral to any attack on urban illiteracy; reports on activities of the Mayor's Commission to recruit students and volunteers.

448. Mayer, Steven E. "Guidelines for Effective Adult Literacy Programs." Bethesda, Maryland: ERIC Document Reproduction Service, ED 268332, 1984.

Describes B. Dalton Booksellers' commitment of funds to increase volunteer participation in eradicating illiteracy, but suggests that staffing can be paid or volunteer depending on the particular goals and needs of the organization involved.

449. Outman, Bob; Ruth Pringle; and Carolyn Latimer. "Allen ISD--Community Education Adult 'Right to Read' Program." Bethesda, Maryland: ERIC Document Reproduction Service, ED 246243, 1984.

Argues that tutors must be professionalized through training, staff development, and recognition. Advocates the use of volunteers as supervisory support for tutors.

450. Parker, Dianne Smith. "The Description and Evaluation of a Peer-Tutoring Program: Implemented and Coordinated by a Parent-Volunteer." Ph.D. dissertation, University of Tennessee, 1984.

Documents the conflicts of a mother attempting to serve as a volunteer, care for her family, and work part-time for pay.

451. Pratt, Fran. "Teaching Today's Kids--Tomorrow's Elders." *Aging*, August/September 1984: 19-26.

Surveys nationwide examples of intergenerational programming at public schools to teach students about aging itself. Six accompanying photographs show men and women volunteers in equal numbers.

452. Rogers, Joy J. "Maintaining Volunteer Participation in Adult Literacy Programs." *Lifelong Learning* 9 (October 1984): 22-4.

Suggests downplaying the idea that literacy can be achieved in measured steps because volunteers may get discouraged and quit.

Recommends instead that volunteer recruiters emphasize how much the volunteer learns from tutoring.

453. Sawyer, Douglas. "ABE Volunteer Recruitment Handbook." Bethesda, Maryland: ERIC Document Reproduction Service, ED 253732, 1984.

Advances the notion that the volunteer instructor should be the student's friend, helper, and counselor as well. Suggests recruiting students by appealing to their sense that ABE is a bargain.

454. "Senior Tutors Help the Public Schools." *Aging*, June/July 1984: 30-1.

States that people over 55 years old should reinforce public school teachers' efforts by volunteering as after-school tutors. Describes RAISE (Retirees Active in Student Education) programs in Michigan and Washington, noting that many RAISE volunteers are themselves retired teachers.

455. Simpson, William M., and C. Russell Koehler. "A Pilot Program to Recruit, Orient, and Use Classroom Volunteers to Assist ABE/ESL Faculty." Bethesda, Maryland: ERIC Document Reproduction Service, ED 246952, 1984.

Addresses the need for community and student-teacher volunteers to assist in overcrowded junior college classrooms.

456. Sizemore, Mamie, ed. "Project SAVE: State Adult Volunteers in Education Organizing a Community-Based Literacy Program." Bethesda, Maryland: ERIC Document Reproduction Service, ED 257937, 1984.

Describes steps involved in organizing a statewide (Laubach) National Affiliation for Literacy Advance program using VISTA volunteers as trainers.

457. Strong, Gary. "Public Libraries and
     Literacy: A New Role to Play." *Wilson
     Library Bulletin* 59 (November 1984): 179-82.

   Discusses available funding for libraries'
literacy projects, citing the Library of
California's decision to set aside $2.5 million in
Library Services and Construction Act (LSCA) funds
for community-based programs using Literacy
Volunteers of America and Laubach volunteers.

458. Taranto, Susanne E., and Simon O. Johnson.
     Educational Volunteerism: A New Look.
     Springfield, Illinois: Thomas, 1984.

   Presents little new information, but does
provide a more scholarly approach, with education
professors and majors the primary audience.
Includes an extensive, detailed chapter listing
twenty-five instruction-oriented volunteer
activities with recommended grade level, goals and
objectives, evaluation, and follow-up activities
for the supervising teacher.

459. Williams, Dennis A. "One-on-One Against
     Illiteracy." *Newsweek,* July 30, 1984, p. 78.

   Notes the centrality of volunteers in
literacy projects but argues that volunteers alone
cannot solve the problem of illiteracy.

1985

460. Baranoff, Timy. "Adopting a School and
     Forming the Future." *The Delta Kappa Gamma
     Bulletin* 51 (Summer 1985): 46-7.

   Describes an Austin, Texas, program wherein
organizations sponsor a school by providing
scholarships, equipment, and volunteer labor.

461. Cooledge, Nancy J., and Stanley R. Wurster.
     "Intergenerational Tutoring and Student
     Achievement." *The Reading Teacher* 39
     (December 1985): 343-6.

Suggests compensating for a dwindling supply of mothers' volunteer labor by enlisting the aid of older Americans. Maintains that tutoring improves reading, citing a study of Arizona State University's Volunteer Partners Program, sixty-four percent female, and its positive effect on boys and girls in Phoenix-area schools.

462. Dawkins, Wayne J. "Fighting Illiteracy." *Black Enterprise*, July 1985, p. 25.

Brief overview of recent efforts to solve the problem of illiteracy among blacks, with information regarding Philadelphia's Mayor's Commission on Literacy and its eighteen hundred volunteers.

463. Endeman, Judith L. "Changing the Generation Gap to a Gain: The Grandpeople Program." *Phi Delta Kappan* 67 (November 1985): 232-3.

Describes a Poway, California, school program relying on older volunteers to tutor, work in libraries and science labs, supervise cooking classes, and serve as oral history sources.

464. Fields, Howard. "Congress Debates Role in Fighting Illiteracy." *Publishers Weekly*, October 18, 1985, p. 20.

Reports on Jonathan Kozol's testimony that volunteers alone cannot eradicate illiteracy but must be augmented with federal dollars.

465. Green, Karen Reed; Stephen Reder; and Nancy Faires Conklin. "Literacy Outreach: The Community Link. A Guide to Working with Literacy Helpers." Bethesda, Maryland: ERIC Document Reproduction Service, ED 263352, 1985.

Recommends recruiting "literacy helpers"--the family members and friends who help the illiterate function in daily life--to become trained volunteer tutors. Argues that this approach eliminates the need to overcome students' resistance.

466. Haley, Virginia. "Redesigning and Expanding the Lower School Parent Volunteer Program to Increase Participation and Participant Satisfaction." Bethesda, Maryland: ERIC Document Reproduction Service, ED 265924, 1985.

Reports the results of questionnaires completed by teachers and parents, including individual comments about the volunteer program at the Lower School of the University School at Nova University in Florida. One respondent commented that recruitment should focus on certified teachers who stayed home with their children. The survey was inspired by teachers' complaints about insufficient numbers of volunteers and their lack of dependability.

467. Hill, Ida J. "Literacy: A Program for Those Who Care." *The Delta Kappa Gamma Bulletin* 51 (Winter-Spring 1985): 5-7.

Maintains that the teaching of illiterates should not be solely the teacher's responsibility but must include unpaid citizens who will tutor, answer telephones, file, and publicize their work.

468. Ilsley, Paul. "Adult Literacy Volunteers: Issues and Ideas." Bethesda, Maryland: ERIC Document Reproduction Service, ED 260303, 1985.

Provides an excellent discussion of the common themes and gaps in the literature primarily of the 1980s, but fails to point out the gender dimension of volunteerism.

469. Kozol, Jonathan. *Illiterate America*. Garden City, New York: Anchor Press/Doubleday, 1985.

Argues that a grassroots movement using volunteer teenagers and senior citizens alongside paid semi-literate poor people should begin expansive literacy education programs, eventually demanding financial support from government.

470. Larson, Marian J. "Parents, Programs and PR." *The Delta Kappa Gamma Bulletin* 51 (Summer 1985): 43-5.

   Describes an Oregon teacher's approach to incorporating mothers into classroom work.

471. McGrath, Mary. "Pint-sized PR." *The Delta Kappa Gamma Bulletin* 51 (Summer 1985): 41-2.

   Maintains that one benefit of involving neighborhood residents as volunteers is their becoming advocates for the school even with "no attempt to indoctrinate them."

472. Meyer, Valerie. "The Adult Literacy Initiative in the U.S.: A Concern and a Challenge." *Journal of Reading* 28 (May 1985): 706-8.

   Addresses concerns of professional teachers who are encouraged to use volunteers for teaching reading in President Reagan's Adult Literacy Initiative of 1983. Suggests that the professional teacher's role is to assist with volunteer training.

473. Minuzzo, Antoinette. "Improving Literacy: A Chapter's Commitment and Involvement." *The Delta Kappa Gamma Bulletin* 51 (Winter/Spring 1985): 8-9.

   Reports on activities of Literacy Volunteers of Lake County, Illinois, originated in 1983 by the Waukegan Public Library adult services coordinator.

474. Rauch, Sidney J., and Joseph Sanacore, eds. *Handbook for the Volunteer Tutor.* 2nd ed. Newark, Delaware: International Reading Association, 1985. (Also available as ED 251817.)

Expresses the belief that tutors must be trained because they work with students who really need professional reading specialists who are not available. Includes nine chapters by various authors.

475. San Diego Urban League. "Basic Education Skills Tutorial (BEST) Program: Report of Second Year July 15, 1985." Bethesda, Maryland: ERIC Document Reproduction Service, ED 273731, 1985.

Addresses the need for tutors of black and minority youth with academic problems; describes a program sponsored by Kappa Alpha Psi Fraternity and San Diego City Schools.

476. South Carolina Department of Education. "Setting up the School Volunteer Program." Bethesda, Maryland: ERIC Document Reproduction Service, ED 262887, 1985.

Gives a basic overview, with a separate section addressing senior citizen volunteers.

477. Valuk, Robert M. "Tutors on Computers." *Phi Delta Kappan* 67 (November 1985): 233.

Describes a Darien, Connecticut, school's use of student tutors and parent monitors in before-school computer labs for second- and third-grade students needing extra math instruction.

1986

478. Arden, Eugene. "Using Volunteers: Colleges Can Learn from Hospitals." *The Chronicle of Higher Education* 63 (July 1986): 613.

Urges universities to use volunteer clerical, science-lab, and library helpers in recognition of the likelihood that budgets will never allow hiring such employees.

479. Bauer, Don. "The Sad Truth About Betty." *Family Circle,* October 1, 1986, p. 48 ff.

Traces a homemaker's turning to Project LEARN in Cleveland for tutoring.

480. "Computer Replaces Volunteers." *Library Journal* 111 (October 15, 1986): 22.

Announces that automation can take over clerical tasks performed by volunteers and notes the use of volunteers for the conversion of records to an automated system.

481. Fischer, Denise R. "Help! I Can't Read: One Librarian's Response." *Texas Library Journal* 62 (Fall 1986): 161.

Proposes the library as the site for volunteer tutoring of illiterates because they see it as a community center rather than associating it with the formal educational system and their own failure to learn.

482. Gaughan, Karen K. "Literacy Projects in Libraries." *Library Trends* 35 (Fall 1986): 277-91.

Supports the use of libraries for Literacy Volunteers of America activities because libraries are non-threatening community centers and librarians' skills enrich the volunteers' efforts.

483. Imel, Susan. "Adult Literacy Volunteers Overview. ERIC Digest No. 48." Bethesda, Maryland: ERIC Document Reproduction Service, ED 268301, 1986.

Surveys items available via ERIC, noting the pros and cons of using volunteers.

484. Karp, Rashelle Schlessinger. "Volunteers in Libraries." In *Advances in Library Administration and Organization: A Research Annual,* Vol. 5, pp. 15-32. Edited by Gerard B. McCabe and Bernard Kreissman. Greenwich, Connecticut: JAI Press, 1986.

Argues that librarians should stop worrying about the disadvantages of exploiting volunteer labor and focus instead on ways to incorporate volunteers into the workforce.

485. "The Key to Literacy--Unlocking Library Doors: A Look at Libraries in NYC Public Elementary Schools." *School Library Journal* (January 1986): 19-21.

Excerpts a study and report by the Citizens' Committee for Children of New York and the Women's City Club of New York demonstrating a trend since 1975 of replacing paid staff with volunteers in and the closing of elementary school libraries.

486. Mathews, Anne J.; Adrienne Chute; and Carol A. Cameron. "Meeting the Literacy Challenge: A Federal Perspective." *Library Trends* 35 (Fall 1986): 219-41.

Lists federally funded programs, many dependent on volunteer labor, available to libraries. Outlines the components of a "model" one-on-one tutoring project using volunteers, based on Renee S. Lerche's *Effective Adult Literacy Programs: A Practitioner's Guide*.

487. Powell, Bob. "Volunteers in the Schools: A Positive Approach to Schooling." *NASSP Bulletin* 70 (December 1986): 32-4.

Argues that the principal must instigate and support the volunteer program if it is to be effective; quotes teachers' glowing praise for unpaid workers.

488. Safran, Claire. "Illiteracy: Read All About It." *Woman's Day*, October 1, 1986, pp. 86-7.

Points the finger at public education for failing to teach all students to read, gives statistics on the cost of "illiteracy-related welfare programs" and concludes with a plea to the magazine's readers to volunteer as tutors.

Promotion of Literacy

489. Sokoloff, Harris J. "School Volunteer Programs." *Media and Methods* 22 (March/April 1986): 39.

   Cites a Houston school volunteer program whose 14,756 participants have donated a half-million hours of service with a resulting increase in student attendance and state funding. Recommends that educators tap the resources of the National School Volunteer Program when setting up local projects.

490. Strong, Gary E. "Adult Literacy: State Library Responses." *Library Trends* 35 (Fall 1986): 243-61.

   Reports on state library efforts to initiate literacy programs, including a detailed discussion of the California Literacy Initiative and its attempt to recruit volunteers more like those needing tutoring, i.e., males, minorities, and youth.

491. U.S. Department of Education. Office of Educational Research and Improvement. "Adult Literacy Programs: Services, Persons Served, and Volunteers." Bethesda, Maryland: ERIC Document Reproduction Service, ED 268387, 1986.

   Reports on the results of a Center for Statistics survey showing that two-thirds of literacy programs use volunteers; tables show the number of volunteers to paid staff and the number of programs managed by volunteers.

492. Weinschenk, D. "I & R Service from Volunteer Senior Citizens." *Library Journal* 111 (October 15, 1986): 50.

   Describes the training of elderly volunteers by the library and social work school instructors at Adelphi University before placement at libraries' information desks.

493. Westreich, Joan. "Why Johnny's Mother Still Can't Read." *Family Circle,* October 1, 1986, p. 46.

Notes that volunteers alone cannot solve the problem of illiteracy and cites funding needs.

494. Young, Christina Carr. "Anatomy of a Technology Transfer: The National Commission on Libraries and Information Science Literacy Project." *Library Trends* 35 (Fall 1986): 263-75.

Describes a pilot program using volunteers and computers to teach language skills at Enoch Pratt Free Library in Baltimore and Mary H. Weir Library in Weirton, West Virginia.

AUTHOR INDEX

(Includes authorship by organizations as well as individuals.)

ACTION 254
ACTION. National
  Student Volunteer
  Program 169, 170,
  222
Adkins, Patricia G.
  255
Ainsworth, Ellen 311
Allen, James E. 113
Allerton Park
  Institute, 25th,
  1979 342
Alloway, Catherine
  Suyak 408
Altshule, Barry 223
American Association
  of Community and
  Junior Colleges.
  Older Americans
  Program 356
American Library
  Association 140
Anderson, A.J. 409
Anderson, Betty 1
Arden, Eugene 478
Armstrong, Audrey A.
  386
Association for
  Childhood Education
  International 76
Atkins, Martin 2
Bahr, Jerome 98
Baker, Diane Haige
  224
Baker, Diane K. 233
Banta, Trudy 357
Baranoff, Timy 460
Barnes, S.A. 256
Bartlett, Robert M. 92
Bartley, Bayard 283
Bassill, Daniel 335
Bauer, Don 479
Baun, Eugene L. 31
Beck, Lillie Adelle
  333

Bell, Afesa M. 319
Bell, Terrel H. 433
Bellassai, Marcia
  Courtney 3435
Bender, L.W. 257
Berclay, G. John 312
Berdeaux, Jack 434
Berg, Paul Conrad 17
Bernstein, Margery R.
  114
Bernstein, Martha 387
Blair, Pat 388
Blankenship, A. Ray
  186
Bloom, Murray Teigh 3
Blume, Libby Balter
  425
Board of Education--
  City of New York
  171
Borden, Jill 434, 435
Boutwell, W.D. 4
Bowman, Georgiana 230
Boyles, Beatrice C.
  56
Brain, Joseph J. 57
Breit, Sally 231
Brentlinger, Howard R.
  26
Brighton, Howard 115,
  172, 173
Brock, Henry C. 284
Brookhart, Norma 174
Brown, Barbara E. 372
Brown, George W. 5
Brown, William C. 383
Burkhardt, Ann Strayer
  32
Burrow, Daniel Alfred
  116.
Cacarillo, Elaine 258
Cameron, Carol A. 486
Caplin, Morris D. 117
Cardenas, Joe A. 58
Carter, Barbara 175,
  225

Carvalho, Joseph 436
Castellucci, Arthur 285
Chambers, Jewell C. 176
Chapman, Alison 389
Chute, Adrienne 486
Clarke, Raymond E. 437
Clough, Bonnie M. 334
Clough, Dick B. 334
Cohen, Royce 118
Cohen, Neal M. 391
Coleman, Jean E. 286
Collins, Michael 339
Columbus, Ohio, City School District 259, 260, 261, 262, 263, 264
Community Services Planning Council 119, 120
Conant, Elizabeth C. 226
Cone, Richard 373
Conklin, Nancy Faires 465
Cooledge, Nancy J. 461
Cooper, Nancy B. 233
Cortright, Richard W. 6, 33
Cory, Christopher T. 227
Coskey, Evelyn 177
Crawford, Mary E. 1
Craymer, Helen S. 77
Criscuolo, Nicholas Paul 142, 178, 179
Curd, David 326
Curry, Anna 411
Dade County (Florida) Public Schools 180
Dade County (Florida) Public Schools. Department of Staff Development 143, 144, 145, 146, 147, 148, 149
Dade County (Florida) Public Schools. School Volunteer Program of Miami 205
Dale, E. Joanne 371
Daly, John H. 438
Damroth, William G. 344
Dapper, Gloria 175, 225
DaSilva, Benjamin 228
Davis, Lorri 439
Dawkins, Wayne J. 462
De Pillis, Susan 374, 392
Deckoff, Marvin J. 412
DeCrow, Roger 181
Delaney, Arthur A. 23
Des Moines Area Community College. Project Motivate 150, 151
Detweiler, Mary Jo 393, 409
Dodson, Kathy 358
Donahue, Mary Marans 78
Douglas, Mary Peacock 7
Doyle, James R. 287
Drennan, Henry T. 61
Eberly, Donald J. 79, 288
Eddison, Elizabeth 251
Eddison, Elizabeth Bole 330
Educational Service Bureau, Inc. 59
Ehda, Patty 370
Eisner, Hannah R. 355

Author Index

Endeman, Judith L. 463
Enk, Jean 294
Erb, Jane 121
Erlich, Sheldon 265
Estroff, Nancy 319
Etlinger, Leonard E. 375
Falik, Louis H. 152
Fay, Leo C. 218
Feeney, Helen M. 182, 307, 337
Fiandt, Bruce 2
Fields, Howard 464
Finacom, Arville 313
Fischer, Denise R. 481
Flanagan, Leo N. 289
Fleming, J. Carl 99
Fleming, Lily 335
Fontaine, Andre 8, 27
Forester, James A. 58
Frazier, Melinda L. 266
Fresno City Unified School District 34
Freund, Janet 35
Fuentes, Martha A. 100
Gartner, Alan 153
Gatchell, Lynn 207
Gaughan, Karen K. 482
Gaulke, Mary F. 183
Gittelson, Natalie 60
Gold, Patricia 267, 290.
Goldring, Cynthia 184
Gonder, Peggy Odell 314
Goodman, Helen C. 185
Goodman, Leroy V. 206
Gordon, Ira J. 122
Goul, Jo 268
Graham, Anne M. 394
Graham, Patricia A. 58

Gray, Sandra T. 440
Green, Karen Reed 465
Greene, Bob 441
Greer, E. 229
Griffin, Bobbie L. 186
Grindstaff, Gordon 376
Groff, Patrick 72
Gross, Melvyn 80
Guinagh, Barry J. 319
Guthrie, Chuck 414
Hadley, Roy E. 315
Haendle, Connie 291, 292
Haley, Virginia 466
Hall, Lee E. 359
Ham, Jane 91
Ham, Wayne 316
Hamm, Ron 125
Hancock, Mary Frank 317
Harmer, Ruth Mulvey 9
Harre, David 81
Harris, Alberta Farmer 442
Harstead, Pat 123, 124
Hartman, Rose Ann 207
Hartman, Rose Anne H. 269
Haugness, Harriette Ellingson 336
Hawkins, Thomas E. 10, 36
Heathman, James E. 154
Helgerson, Linda 230
Helgerson, Linda W. 293
Hendricks, Meg 294
Hettling, Lillian B. 415
Hiatt, Peter 61
Hickey, Howard W. 208
Hickey, Margaret 11

Hickman, Charles W. 187
Hill, Corrine Paxman 360
Hill, Ida J. 467
Hillenbrand, Robert F. 62
Hoffman, Catherine N. 368
Hooper, Richard 295
Hoot, James L. 416
Hopkins, Lee Bennnett 70
Horrell, Sallie 417
Hospodar, J. 215
Howard, Leon 348
Hubley, John W. 188
Hunt, Sally P. 386
Hunter, Madeline 231
Iacolucci, Grace M. 82
Illinois Office of Education 296
Ilsley, Paul 337, 339, 377, 468
Imel, Susan 483
Industrial and Business Training Bureau. Division of Extension. The University of Texas at Austin 232
Institute for Development of Educational Activities (Dayton, Ohio) 189, 190
Jackson, Audrey 270
Jackson, Audrey H. 233
Jackson, Jr., Maxie C. 191
Jamer, T. Margaret 20
Janey, Jane 419
Janowitz, Gayle 28, 37, 83, 155

Jarlsberg, Jane 306
Jenkins, Harold 192
Jensen, Mary Dodd 125
Jensen, Pauline L. 64
Johnson, Judith 373
Johnson, Laura 39
Johnson, Simon O. 319, 458
Johnson, Vance O'Neal 420
Jordan, William C. 84
Kagan, Sharon Lynn 421
Karant, Vicki I. 320
Karp, Rashelle Schlessinger 484
Keegan, Francis W. 156
Keller, M. Jean 422
Kellogg, Larry James 361
Keltz, Dave 126
Kennison, Pat 321
Kies, Cosette 297
Klebaner, Ruth Perlman 65
Klopf, Gordon 1
Koehler, C. Russell 443, 444, 445, 455
Kohler, Mary Conway 153
Koretsky, Edna 127
Kornblau, Esther 346
Kozol, Jonathan 362, 363, 469
Kozoll, Charles E. 193
Kruuse, Myrna 346
Kuras, Christine 271
Lancaster County, Pennsylvania, Library 209
Lancaster, Joyce 353
Lander, Faye 423
Lane, Martha A. 446
Larson, Marian J. 470

Latimer, Carolyn 449
Laubach, Frank C. 128
Laubach, Robert S. 128
Lawson, Sandra S. 357
Lea, William Lowell 234
Leaf, Berniece 39
LeBoeuf, Flores 85
LeClair-Marzolf, Marsha 378
Lee, Calvin B.T. 38
Leedom, JoAnne 157
Leggette, Earl C. 348
Leppert, Alice 339
Levenson, Dorothy 66
Levine, Ellen 364
LeVine, Evelyn 194, 210
Lippitt, Peggy 101
Literacy Volunteers of America, Inc. 235, 273
Lockhart, John 158
Logan, George King 12
Long, Helen Halter 13
Longeway, B. 349
Los Angeles City Schools. Office of Urban Affairs 86
Los Angeles City Unified School District 211
Los Angeles City Unified School District. Volunteer and Tutorial Programs 212
Lovelace, Terry 365
Lucas, Linda 366
Lucas, Richard D. 228
Lund, Arline 159
Lyman, Helen Huguenor 322
MacDonald, Bernice 49
MacLean, Jean Ann 156

Maerowitz, Inge 213
Malarkey, Didi 195
Mallery, D. 50
Massachusetts Council for Public Schools, Inc. Project for Adult Literacy 102
Massey, Jeanne H. 275
Mastors, Charlotte 276
Mathews, Anne J. 486
Matley, Marcel B. 196
Mattleman, Marciene S. 447
Mayer, Steven E. 448
McCauley, Elfrieda 299
McCracken, Robert A. 39
McGrath, Mary 471
McGuire, Agnes C. 236
McKinley, Carey 396
Melaragno, Ralph J. 103
Mesa, Pete 367
Meyer, Valerie 472
Miller, Bette L. 277
Milligan, Bill 126
Minuzzo, Antoinette 473
Montgomery (Alabama) Community Action Agency 160
Moon, Eric 87
Moore, Roberta J. 197
Moss, Jeanette K. 237
Motzkus, John E. 88
Moussa, Linda 301
Mulligan, Dorothy 350
Musar, Norma 95
Myers, Jean Davis 275
Nagle, Terry Lynne 380
National Commission on Resources for Youth 238

National School
 Volunteer Program
 338, 379
Naylor, Harriet N.
 356
New York City School
 Volunteer Program,
 Inc. 171
Newman, A. P. 397
Newmark, Gerald 103
Newton, Eunice Shaed
 40
Nielsen, Wilhemine R.
 89
Niemi, John A. 339,
 377
Norton, Michael M.
 214
Norton, Eloise 41
Nyren, Karl 161, 398
O'Banner, B. Marie
 348
O'Connell, Carol 278
O'Connell, Carol
 Patricia 323
Ogletree, Earl J. 375
Opportunities
 Industrialization
 Centers of America,
 Inc. 199
Orange County
 (California)
 Department of
 Education 162
Osborne, Pearl 1
Outman, Bob 449
Owens, LaVerne 442
Palzer, Doris M. 279,
 324
Panek, Alice 200
Paramore, B. 215
Parker, Dianne Smith
 450
Parrish, William C.
 381

Parten, Carroll B.
 129
Pearson, David A. 131
Peckham, Earl K. 14
Perkins, Bryce 51
Petgen, Elizabeth A.
 52
Phinney, Eleanor 15
Pines, Maya 21
Plantec, B. 215
Powell, Bob 487
Powell, Conrad 310
Pratt, Fran 451
President's Commission
 on the Status of
 Women, The 24
Pringle, Ruth 449
Project VOICE 163
Provus, Malcolm 68
Purcell, Elizabeth A.
 380
Raim, Joan 216
Rauch, Sidney J. 104,
 474
Recruitment Leadership
 and Training
 Institute 280
Reder, Stephen 465
Reed, Betty Jane 69
Regional Conference
 for College Social
 Service
 Organizations.
 Cornell University
 90
Reynolds, Mary I. 281
Rich, Leslie 217
Ridge, Aldema A. 401
Riessman, Frank 153
Riley, Mary Tom 425
Rime, Laura 91
Robb, Mel H. 105
Roedder, Kathleen R.
 42
Rogers, Joy J. 452

Author Index

Rothschild, Mary Aickin 402
Rubin, Lois 230
Ryan, Jamice 241
Safran, Claire 488
Sainer, Janet S. 164
Salisbury, Robert H. 325
San Bruno Park (California) School District. Curricular Services Center 303
San Diego Urban League 475
Sanacore, Joseph 474
Sannwald, William W. 368
Savage, Noel 304, 305
Sawyer, Douglas 453
Schraft, Carol 421
Schmidt, Susan K. 242
Schmitz, Paul 194, 210
Schoeller, Arthur W. 131
Schulte, Jean Kendall 427
Scullen, Thomas 326
Sekowsky, Jo Anne 132
Seney, Heidi 243
Sequin, Mary M. 306
Shalen, Marcia 53
Shapiro, Annette Frank 70
Shelley, Florence D. 75
Shipp, Mary E. 71
Shourts, John L. 348
Shue, D.E. 54
Simpson, William M. 455
Sindledecker, Charles 133
Sizemore, Mamie 456
Skjoiten, Mae 92
Slack, Georgia 340

Slater, Marcia 352
Sleisenger, Lenore 43, 353
Smith, Brenda 230
Smith, Carl B. 218
Smith, Ester Gottlieb 382
Smith, Mildred B. 134
Sokoloff, Harris J. 489
South Carolina Department of Education 476
Stahl, Norman A. 383
Staley, Gerald J. 135
Stanton, Vida C. 341
Stavros, Denny 165
Steeger, Henry 106
Stenzel, Anne K. 307
Stephan, Sandra 308
Stoker, Linda 335
Stone, Eve M. 339
Stone, Marvin 428
Stone, Virginia 93
Stouffer, Russell G. 72
Stradley, William E. 73
Streit, John F. 282
Strong, Gary 457, 490
Swanker, Esther M. 25
Swanson, Mary. T. 136
Talbot, Virginia 137
Taltavull, Frances Adeline 244
Taranto, Susanne E. 403, 458
Taylor, Adele M. 267
Thelen, Herbert A. 107
Thomas, S. Louise 74
Thompson, Diane D. 166
Thurber, John C. 219
Tierce, Jerry Wood 404

Tobin, Michael F. 166
Trainer, Leslie 309
Trasin, Walter 18
Troutner, Joan 95
True, Douglas 370
Tucker, Marjorie P. 220
Tunick, Adele B. 45
U.S. Department of Education. Office of Educational Research and Improvement 491
U.S. Department of Health, Education, and Welfare. Office of Citizen Participation 138
U.S. Department of Health, Education, and Welfare. Office of Education 245, 246, 247
U.S. Department of Labor. Manpower Administration 109
Valuk, Robert M. 477
Venner, Herb 123, 124
Waite, Peter A. 430
Warmbrod, Catharine P. 355
Warner, Alice Sizer 202, 251, 330, 431
Warner, Ruth 252
Washington Technical Institute. Division of Research and Development 167
Watman, Thomas J. 55
Weed, Florence C. 110
Weinschenk, D. 492
Welliver, M. Margaret 432
Westreich, Joan 493
Wexler, Sandra 152
Whaley, Nita B. 221

White, Annadale Rhoads 331
Willey, Lawrence 46
Williams, Billie 371
Williams, Dennis A. 459
Williams, Polly Franklin 253
Wilmshurst, Ann L. 277
Winecoff, Larry 310
Wolf, Elinor 97
Wolman, Thelma G. 75
Wood, Janice 384
Wood, W.R. 16
Wright, Benjamin 19
Wright, Betty Atwell 112
Wright, Elizabeth J. 47
Wurster, Stanley R. 461
Wyckoff, Lorna M. 332
Wynn, Louisia B. 233
Young, Christina Carr 494
Zander, Mary L. 164

TITLE INDEX

ABC's ... A Handbook for Educational Volunteers 176
"ABC's of Courage: At Day's End, One Man Learns That He Can Learn, The" 441
"ABE Volunteer Recruitment Handbook" 453
"Administrative Practices Employed by Principals in Selected School Volunteer Programs" 336
"Administrators' Forum--Readers' Choice" 48
Administrator's Guide to the Use of Volunteer Teachers 193
"Administrator's Workshop: Volunteer On-the-Job Training Pays Off, The" 139
"Adopting a School and Forming the Future" 460
Adult Learner: A Handbook for Volunteer and New Adult Education Teachers, The 434
"Adult Learner Services at the Pratt Library: An Evaluative Treatment" 411
"Adult Literacy Classes in Public Library" 54
"Adult Literacy Initiative in the U.S.: A Concern and a Challenge, The " 472
"Adult Literacy Programs: Services, Persons Served, and Volunteers" 491
"Adult Literacy: State Library Responses" 490
"Adult Literacy Volunteers: Issues and Ideas" 468
"Adult Literacy Volunteers Overview. ERIC Digest No. 48" 483
"Adult School in Suburban Los Angeles Fills Community Education Roles" 223
After School Study Centers: Experimental Materials and Clinical Research. Final Report 83
"After-School Study Centers: Volunteer Work in Reading" 28
"Aides Acquire Marketable Skills" 423
Aides to Teachers and Children 76
"ALA and Other Members of Coalition for Literacy Announce $1.7 Million Goal" 385
"Allen ISD--Community Education Adult 'Right to Read' Program" 449
"Alley Library, The" 81

Americans Volunteer 109

Americans Volunteer--1974 254

"Anatomy of a Technology Transfer: The National Commission on Libraries and Information Science Literacy Project" 494

"And Whom Have I Done What For?" 297

"Another New Force" 206

"Assignment: Administrative Volunteer" 308

Assisting in the Classroom. An Individualized Volunteer Education Module 143

"Back-up Brigade: Volunteer Tutors Lend a Hand" 376

"Barriers to Voluntarism" 195

"Basic Education Skills Tutorial (BEST) Program: Report of Second Year July 15, 1985" 475

"Bears and Butterflies: The Literacy Volunteers of Gloucester (Virginia). Project POWER, 1982-83" 417

Because They Care: A Resource Manual for Volunteer Programs 296

Becoming a School Volunteer. An Individualized Volunteer Education Module 144

"Becoming Community Participants" 1

"'Before' You Begin: Feasibility of Aged Volunteers Tutoring Children in Reading" 365

"Better Reading Through Volunteer Reading Tutors" 131

Beyond the Ivory Tower: Social Responsibility and the College Student 90

"Big Business Comes to the Aid of Recruitment" 204

"Boise Likes its School Volunteers" 268

Building One to One Relationships. An Individualized Volunteer Education Module 145

"Can Learners Teach?" 18

"Case Study of an Educational Change Effort: The Organization and Implementation of a Community Volunteer Program at Piedmont Middle School, A" 420

"Changing the Generation Gap to a Gain: The

Title Index 125

Grandpeople Program" 463
"Children Can Teach Other Children" 101
"Children Computer Volunteers Help Janesville, Wisc. Program" 410
Children Teach Children: Learning by Teaching 153
"'Chronicles'--An Intergenerational Experience" 415
"Citizen Participation in the Public Schools" 325
"Classroom Supervision of Volunteers: Handbook for Instructors" 443
"Clearinghouse for Maryland Volunteers" 390
"College Students Become Teachers' Helpers" 58
"Columbia College Citizenship Program, The" 38
"Commentary: Examining Volunteer Expenses" 349
"Community Link: Libraries and the Literacy Volunteers of America, The" 291
"Community Responsibility for Literacy Education" 16
"Community-Run Library Attempts to Raise Funds" 141

"Comparative Descriptive Study of Michigan State University Student Volunteers and the Relationship of Their Background and Individual Characteristics to Student Activists and to Non-Student Volunteers, A" 191
"Comparative Study of Formal Volunteer Programs in Educational Settings, A" 360
"Compliments of the Service Gents" 88
"Computer Replaces Volunteers" 480
"Congress Debates Role in Fighting Illiteracy" 464
"Cooperation/ Volunteers" 161
"Coordinator's 'How to Do' Handbook, A" 163
"Description and Evaluation of a Peer-Tutoring Program: Implemented and Coordinated by a Parent-Volunteer, The" 450
"Developing a School Volunteer Program" 319
"Developing Parent Commitment to Public Education: New Directions for the 1980's" 421

"Development and
  Implementation of a
  Multi-Purpose School
  Volunteer Program in
  an Adult Education
  Center" 361
"Development of a
  Model Program for
  the Recruitment,
  Training, and
  Utilization of
  Elderly School
  Volunteers, The"
  437
"Digging for Human
  Treasure" 287
"Do-It-Yourself: The
  Grandpeople Project"
  374
"Docents at Los
  Angeles Public: An
  Elite Volunteer
  Guide Corps" 413
"Early Childhood
  Education: How to
  Organize Volunteers;
  How and Where to
  Find Volunteers"
  211
"Educational Roles for
  Volunteer Youth"
  155
*Educational
  Volunteerism: A New
  Look* 458
"Effect of an
  Instructional
  Volunteer Program on
  an Elementary
  School, The" 282
*Effective Involvement
  of School Volunteers*
  350
"Effective Utilization
  of Volunteers in
  Head Start Programs:
  A Manual" 419
"Effects of a
  Volunteer Tutor
  Program on Self-
  Esteem and Basic
  Skills Achievement
  in the Primary
  Grades of a Southern
  Rural School System"
  316
"Effects of Different
  Volunteer
  Tutor/Tutee
  Combinations on the
  Reading and
  Mathematics
  Achievement and Self
  Concept of
  Elementary Tutees"
  224
"Elementary Principal
  Views the Feminine
  Mystique, An" 62
"Elementary School
  Volunteers" 156
"Establishing Right to
  Read Programs in
  Community-Based
  Adult Learning
  Centers" 232
"Evaluation of the
  Lenoir City
  (Tennessee) Schools
  Retirement Power in
  Education Project,
  1979-1980" 357
*Evaluation of the
  School Volunteers
  Project, 1970-1, The*
  165
"Examination of
  Volunteers and
  Attitudes Toward
  Education, An" 427

Title Index

"Expanding Volunteers in Teaching and Learning Programs. An I/D/E/A Occasional Paper" 189
"Factors Related to Implementation of Programs of Parent Volunteer Classroom Involvement in Selected Elementary Schools of Florida" 317
"Fairly Boring Jobs for Young People" 378
"Fighting Illiteracy" 462
"Final Teacher Training (Staff Development) Project Report for Volunteer Adult Basic Reading Tutorial Program" 273
"The Force: Middle School Style" 401
Four Consultations 24
"Franklin Elementary School Tutorial Enrichment Program in Elementary Education" 442
Getting Better Results from Substitutes, Teacher Aides, and Volunteers 51
Getting People to Read: Volunteer Programs That Work 218
Good Friends Volunteer Program Evaluation Report, The 295

"Good Students Help Deficient Pupils" 23
"Grandpersons Wanted Here!" 345
"Guide for Organizing a Volunteer Adult Reading Program (VARP), A" 414
Guide for Volunteers in Mathematics 158
Guidebook for the Volunteer Reading Teacher (1965) 43, (1979) 353
"Guidelines for Effective Adult Literacy Programs" 448
"Guidelines for Involving Older School Volunteers" 338
"Guidelines for Using Volunteers in Libraries" 140
"Haaren's Miracles" 258
"Handbook for Library Volunteers" 303
Handbook for Teacher Aides 173
Handbook for the Volunteer Tutor (1969) 104; (1985) 474
"Handbook for Utilizing Volunteer Tutors in an Adult Basic Education Program, A" 432
"Handbook for Volunteer Coordinators of ABE/ESL Classroom Volunteers" 444

Handbook for Volunteer Reading Aides (1972) 174
Handbook for Volunteer Reading Aides (1984) 446
Handbook for Volunteers, A 146
"Handbook for Volunteers: Adult Education Program" 445
"Harnessing Volunteer Energy in a Community Library" 196
"'Hart Day': Parents Take Over So Teachers Can Attend a Guidance Conference" 77
"Help! I Can't Read: One Librarian's Response" 481
"Help is Out There--Here's How to Find It" 383
"Help! The Answer Can Be Volunteers" 358
Helping Hands: Volunteer Work in Education 37
Helping Students Develop Appropriate Behavior. An Individualized Volunteer Education Module 147
High School Courses with Volunteer Components 222
High School Student Volunteers 170
"How Do You Manage? Why Not Volunteers?" 409

"How the Profession Feels About Teacher Aides" 63
"How to Create a Successful School/Community Partnership" 440
"How to Cut Costs by Using Unpaid Volunteers" 184
How to Organize a School Volunteer Program in Individual Schools and Suggested Volunteer Aids 86
"How to Put Parents to Work in the Classroom" 84
"How We Can Win: A Plan to Reach and Teach Twenty-Five Million Illiterate Adults" 362
"Hurst, Texas, Volunteers Save Library $165,000" 418
"I & R Service from Volunteer Senior Citizens" 492
"Idea Exchange: Volunteerism" 241
"Identification of Major Competencies and Attributes Needed by Volunteer Literacy Tutors of Adults and the Development of a Tutor Self-Assessment Inventory, The" 372
"If You Love Me in the Fall, Will You Keep

Me 'til Spring?" 318
"Illiteracy at the Crossroads" 17
"Illiteracy: Read All About It" 488
Illiterate America 469
"Implementing Volunteer Services within a School" 290
"Improving Literacy: A Chapter's Commitment and Involvement" 473
"In Minneapolis: Hundreds of Volunteers Help Teachers Teach Better" 64
"Individualizing Reading with Pupil-Teachers" 39
Information for the Volunteer Tutor 160
"Inside to Outside and Back Again" 52
"Interest Stimulators" 93
"Intergenerational Tutoring and Student Achievement" 461
"Invaluable Resource: The School Volunteer, An" 117
"Investigation of the Effect of Volunteer Tutors and Readers on Reading Achievement of Fifth-Grade Pupils in an Inner-City School, An" 244
"Investigation of Volunteer and Nonvolunteer Parents Concerning Students' Reading Achievement and Attendance, An" 333
"Investing in a Talent Bank" 344
"Issues and Legislation Related to Volunteer Utilization in Public Schools" 315
"Key to Literacy--Unlocking Library Doors: A Look at Libraries in NYC Public Elementary Schools, The" 485
"Laubach Trained Volunteer Tutor Pilot Project 1971" 183
"Leader Behaviors, Leader Styles, and Management Effectiveness of Elementary Teachers as Related to Paid Teacher Aides and Volunteer Teacher Aides" 323
"Legal Status of Volunteers Clarified in Florida" 347
"Letters" 266
Libraries and Literacy: A Summary Report 343
Libraries in Literacy 382
"Libraries of All Types Depending on Volunteers" 272
Library Adult Education in Action:

Five Case Studies 15
"Library and Literacy Eduction in the '80's" 408
"Library Volunteer--I: Voluntarism and Librarianship, The" 202
"Library Volunteer--II: Volunteers in the Future of Libraries, The" 192
"Library Volunteer--III: Volunteers in El Paso, The" 185
"Lighten Your Load with Volunteers: A Guide for Teachers, Administrators, Parents, and Community Volunteers" 294
Linking Schools and the Community 314
"Linking Up through LINKS" 157
"'Listening Mothers'" 74
"Literacy: A Program for Those Who Care" 467
Literacy Activities in Public Libraries: A Report of a Study of Services to Adult Illiterates 49
Literacy and the Nation's Libraries 322
Literacy: Meeting the Challenge: The Private Sector Involvement in Literacy Efforts 335

"Literacy Outreach: The Community Link. A Guide to Working with Literacy Helpers" 465
"Literacy Programs, Library" 286
"Literacy Projects in Libraries" 482
"Little Extra Push: School Volunteer Program" 21
"LJ: News" 298
"LSCA-funded Volunteer Program Catches on in Carroll County" 395
"Magic Ingredient of Volunteerism" 217
"Maintaining Volunteer Participation in Adult Literacy Programs" 452
"Manpower: A Soviet Solution?" 87
"Manual for a Volunteer Services System" 230
"Manual for Developing a Senior Citizen Teacher Aide Program" 274
"Mayor's Commission on Literacy in Philadelphia. Final Narrative/Report" 447
"Medford Storytelling Guild: or Volunteers, Unlimited" 388
"Meeting the Literacy Challenge: A Federal Perspective" 486
"Men Volunteers Tops" 424

"METRO Studies Volunteer Use; Tucson Urges Program" 300
"METRO Workshop on Volunteers in Libraries Sparks Controversy, Offers Practical Advice" 309
"Model for a Volunteer Teacher Aide Program, A" 234
"Mothers Bring Their Skills to School" 66
"National Right to Read Effort, The" 198
"National Right to Read Partners" 181
"Need for Volunteers Cited: New Projects Reported" 239
"Need Help on Those Local 'Drives'? Enlist the Teens!" 3
Neighborhood Study Center Teacher Aide Program: 1969-1970 Evaluation, The 119
"New Branches Grow on the Educational Family Tree" 56
New Roles for Youth in the School and the Community 238
"New York City School Volunteer Program, The" 171
"News and Comment: Should Children Teach?" 19
"News Report 1975" 304

"No Trained Teachers for Foreign Languages?" 5
"Non-Professional Teachers Enliven the Subject Matter" 98
"Of Course, Volunteers" 267
"Older Adult Volunteers" 416
"On the Care and Feeding of Volunteers" 25
"One-on-One Against Illiteracy" 459
"One Volunteer Experiment" 240
"'Open-to-the-World' School, An" 237
"Operating a Retirees Volunteer Program in Postsecondary Institutions: A Resource Handbook" 355
Organizational Management Handbook 292
Organizing a Volunteer Program 310
Organizing School Volunteer Programs 225
Organizing the Library's Support: Donors, Volunteers, Friends 342
"Organizing Volunteers Statewide: Florida Raises an Army of Able Helpers for the State's Students and Teachers Through an Organized and Efficient Statewide

School Volunteer
Program" 403
"Parent Aides for
Public Kindergarten
... A Pilot Project"
95
*Parent Involvement in
Compensatory
Education* 122
"Parent Involvement in
Schools: A Parent's
View" 311
"Parent Involvement in
the Classroom: Boon
or Bane" 255
*Parent Involvement in
the Schools* 312
"Parent Power at
Pennwood Junior
High" 279
"Parent Volunteer
Handbook: Teachers
Need Parents--
Parents Need
Teachers--Students
Need Both" 370
*Parent Volunteer
Programs in Early
Childhood Education:
A Practical Guide*
284
"Parent Volunteers:
Crucial Helpers"
321
*Parents and Volunteers
in the Classroom: A
Handbook for
Teachers* 277
"Parents as Listeners"
132
"Parents as Teachers
Aides" 82
"Parents! Bless Them
and Keep Them ... In
Your Classroom" 213

"Parents Enrich
Classroom Program"
89
"Parents, Programs and
PR" 470
"Partners for
Literacy" 118
"Patterns of Volunteer
Service by Young
People: 1965 and
1974" 288
"People Are Your Most
Valuable Resources"
399
"Personality
Differences Between
Volunteers and
Professionals" 78
*Philosophical Approach
for Volunteers, A*
253
"Pilot Program to
Recruit, Orient, and
Use Classroom
Volunteers to Assist
ABE/ESL Faculty, A"
455
"Pint-Size Tutors
Learn by Teaching"
67
"Pint-Sized PR" 471
*Place for Everyone:
Higher Education and
the Older Volunteer,
A* 356
"Plan, Polish, Promote
and Practice a
School Volunteer
Program" 233
"Potential Building
Technique (PBT): A
Volunteer Para-
Professional for the
Classroom" 283
"PR Program Runs
Farther, Faster with

Title Index

Volunteer People Power!" 214
Practical School Volunteer and Teacher-Aide Programs 228
"Practicing Librarians: Volunteerism in Ventura County" 368
Prisoners of Silence: Breaking the Bonds of Adult Illiteracy in the United States 363
"Proceedings of the Right to Read: The Role of the Volunteer" 130
"Profile of a Literacy Teacher" 33
"Project Reachout" 278
"Project SAVE: State Adult Volunteers in Education Organizing a Community-Based Literacy Program" 456
"Project to Utilize Volunteers in Eliminating Adult Illiteracy: Butte, Montana" 126
"Project to Utilize Volunteers in Eliminating Adult Illiteracy. Quarterly Progress Report. First Quarter." 123.
"Project to Utilize Volunteers in Eliminating Adult Illiteracy. Quarterly Report. Second Quarter." 124
"Project Upswing After Two Years: An Evaluation" 215
Project VUE: Volunteers Upholding Education 219
"Proposition 13 Spurs Use of Volunteers in Ventura" 351
"Providence Library Gets $$ to Establish Volunteer Program" 400
"PTA--Library Supporter, The" 42
"Public Libraries and Literacy: A New Role to Play" 457
Public Library Services for the Functionally Illiterate: A Survey of Practice 61
Pupil Assistant in the School Library, The 7
"Pupil-Teachers" 70
"Pupil Tutors and Tutees Learn Together" 99
"Qui Docet Discit--He Who Teachers, Learns" 85
"Rationale and Recommendations for Using Retired Citizens as Volunteers in Public Schools, A" 281
"Rationale for Community Volunteers in Schools" 367
"Reading in High Gear" 46

"Reading Moms: A Program that Works" 326
"Reading: Teaching Migrant Children" 159
"Reading, Writing, Rithmetic--and Love" 100
"Recruit 'Grandpeople' as Volunteer Tutors, and Students Will Reap the Rewards" 392
Recruiting and Training Volunteers 377
"Recruiting, Training, Utilizing, and Evaluating Volunteers" 208
"Redesigning and Expanding the Lower School Parent Volunteer Program to Increase Participation and Participant Satisfaction" 466
"Released Time for Inservice Teachers? Try Volunteers (University Professors)" 348
"Remarkable Story of the Dropouts and the College Students, The" 27
"Reports on Management of Seven Common Chronic Library Problems as Summarized by Facilitators of Discussion Groups at the Fall 1975 and Spring 1976 Meetings of the Wisconsin Library Association Children's and Young People's Services Section" 302
"Reveille for Volunteers" 97
Right to Read: The Role of the Volunteer, The 113
"Role of the Secondary School Volunteer as Perceived by School Volunteer Coordinators, The" 404
"Role of the Southern Appalachian Public Library in Dealing with Functional Illiteracy, The" 177
"Role of the Volunteer, The" 57
"Role of the Volunteer Teacher" 128
"Role of Volunteers in Adult Literacy Programs, The" 430
"Rolling Out the Welcome Mat to Tutors" 216
"RSVP: A Resource for Volunteers" 324
"Sad Truth About Betty, The" 479
"San Diego Volunteers Rate $5 an Hour" 426
"School and Community--Partners in Education" 201
"School Libraries and Volunteer Help" 41

Title Index

"School Resources Volunteer Story: Berkeley, California" 125
"School Volunteer Program, The" 53
"School Volunteer Program: A Resource for the Schools" 375
"School Volunteer Program: A Two-Year Evaluation Report" 369
"School Volunteer Program. Progress Report September 15, 1971-June 15, 1972" 180
"School Volunteer Programs" 489
School Volunteer Programs: Everything You Need to Know to Start or Improve Your Program 379
School Volunteer Programs ... How They Are Organized and Managed 188
"School Volunteer Project in Boston, The" 127
"School Volunteers: A New Challenge" 65
"School Volunteers and Early Childhood Education (Community Involvement)" 212
School Volunteers: Creating a New Dimension in Education Through Lay Participation: Including the History of the First

School Volunteer Program 20
School Volunteers: Districts Recruit Aides to Meet Rising Costs, Student Needs 221
"School Volunteers Face the Issues" 332
"School Volunteers: Vital Resource in a Troubled Time" 313
School Volunteers: What They Do, How They Do It 175
School Volunteers: Who Needs Them? 276
"School's More Fun When Parents Help Teach" 8
"Schools and Volunteers" 387
"Season of Helping, A" 22
"Second Pair of Hands: School Volunteer Program" 60
"Senior Readers in the Elementary Library" 439
"Senior Tutors Help the Public Schools" 454
"SERVE: Older Volunteers in Community Service. A New Role and a New Resource" 164
"Service Experience and Educational Growth" 79
"Setting up the School Volunteer Program" 476

"Sharing of Life and Learning--An Intergenerational Program, The" 422
"Should You Use Pupil Tutors?" 72
"Sixth-Grade Tutors" 91
"Socrates Denied: A Defeat for Community Resources People in the Public Schools" 320
"Some Second Thoughts on Survival in the Seventies: Or Two Views of the Volunteer Dilemma" 289
"Something More" 50
"Springfield School Volunteers" 121
Staffing for Better Schools (Under Title I, Elementary and Secondary Education Act of 1965) 68
"Student Tutors for Floundering Classmates" 29
Student Volunteers: A Manual for Communities 169
"Student Volunteers as Group Leaders in Elementary Schools" 92
"Study of the Effects of Trained vs. Untrained Volunteer Aides in Individualized Reading Instruction in Grade Five, A" 331

"Summer Tutoring: An Investigation of Older Volunteer Students Tutoring Younger Students in Arithmetic Computation" 116
"SVP Leader's Handbook" 205
"Task Forces for Planning ACTION Volunteer Use in Adult Basic Education: A Mechanism for Promoting Innovation in ABE. Final Report" 199
"Teacher Aides" 137
"Teacher Aides: A Survey" 71
"Teacher Aides to the Rescue: Program Guidelines for Better Home-School-Community Partnerships" 112
Teacher Assistants: A Blueprint for a Successful Volunteer-Aide Program 105
"Teacher Who Did, A" 252
"Teacher: Your Neighborhood is a Wealth of Help" 346
"Teacher's 'Big' Helper" 80
"Teachers for a Day" 2
"Teaching Adults to Read: Research and Demonstration in a Program of Volunteer

Title Index

Community Action" 102
"Teaching Today's Kids--Tomorrow's Elders" 451
"TEAM Volunteers Cut School Failures" 94
"Ten Proven Programs to Prevent Dropouts" 44
"Thank You for Coming! Minneapolis Schools Welcome Volunteers in Their Community Resource Program" 69
"They Are Learning to Read" 6
"They Can't Say No" 108
"Thoughts on the Teacher Aide Program" 115
"Three Chances to Help" 428
"Three R's and an S For Service" 9
"Time and Knowledge to Share" 35
"To Complement or Compete? The Role of Volunteers in Public Libraries" 436
"To Educate Children Effectively We Must Involve Parents" 134
"Toward a Learning Society" 433
"Toward More Effective Involvement of the Community in the School. An Occasional Paper" 190

"Trained Volunteer and the Elementary Library, The" 32
"Training and Use of Volunteer Recruiters in Adult Basic Education Programs. Alabama III (Huntsville) Module. Final Report" 186
"Training Program for Volunteers, A" 129
"Training the Volunteer Reading Tutor" 40
"Training Tutors Effectively" 142
"Troubled Schools Turn to Volunteer Helpers" 327
"Tutorial Community Works Toward Specific Objectives in an Elementary School, A" 103
"Tutorial Program: What Kind of Answer to the Problem of Academic Deficiency in the Urban Minority Group Community, The" 152
"Tutoring by Students" 107
Tutoring in Reading and Mathematics. An Individualized Volunteer Education Module 148
"Tutoring Programs: School Volunteers in New Haven" 178
Tutoring Resource Handbook for Teachers. A Guide for Teachers Who Are

Working with Volunteer Reading Tutors 245
Tutoring Techniques for Use in Neighborhood Study Centers. Neighborhood Study Center and Teacher Aide Program: Volunteer Guide 120
Tutor-Trainers' Resource Handbook: Part A--Reading Directors' Organizational Guidelines; Part B--Tutor-Trainers' Guidelines; Part C--Teacher-orientation Guidelines 247
Tutor's Guidebook for Remedial Reading, A 179
"Tutors on Computers" 477
Tutors' Resource Handbook: Assessment Items and Sample Lessons 246
"Two Generations of Volunteers: Grandparents" 243
"Two Generations of Volunteers: Parents" 227
"Unpaid Volunteers Pay Off for Inner-City Schools" 166
"Upper-graders Learn by Teaching" 47
"Using Community Assets for Better Learning: College Students Can Help" 197

"Using Community Resources to Improve the First Grade Experience: Project Upswing. A Summary" 248
Using the Services of a School Volunteer. An Individualized Volunteer Education Module 149
"Using Volunteers: Colleges Can Learn from Hospitals" 478
"Using Volunteers in Compensatory Education" 34
"Utilize an Untapped Resource" 438
Utilizing Teacher Aides in Differentiated Staffing 172
Utilizing Teacher Aides in the Classroom 334
"Utilizing the Services of the Academically Talented Students" 36
Utilizing Volunteers to Expand Services to Disadvantaged Adults 242
"Vintage Volunteers in the Library" 306
"VIPs in 'VIP', The" 265
VITAL Guidelines. Tutor Training for an Adult Literacy Program 386
"Voluntarism: An Action Proposal for

Adult Educators" 337
"Voluntarism at the Crossroads: A Challenge for Adult Educators" 339
"Voluntarism in the Volunteer State" 269
"Volunteer Adult Basic Reading Tutorial Program: Final Special Demonostration Project Report" 235
"Volunteer Aides" 200
"Volunteer Aides Handbook: Media Center" 162
"Volunteer Aides in Public Schools: Policies and Procedures in Oregon and Washington" 135
"Volunteer Aides in the Reading Room" 256
"Volunteer and Professional--The Role of Adult Education" 182
"Volunteer--An Educational Resource, The" 154
Volunteer Assistance in the Library 271
"Volunteer Efforts Recongized at Laramie County" 396
"Volunteer Grandparents in Head Start" 425
"Volunteer Help: Resource in Instruction?" 187

"Volunteer: Key to Community-Based Education" 257
"Volunteer: Key to Successful Fund-Raising, The" 412
"Volunteer Mother Program" 285
"Volunteer Mothers as Tutors in the Classroom" 275
"Volunteer Mothers Ease Teacher's Task" 133
"Volunteer Participation in the Functioning of the Howland Circulating Library, Beacon, New York" 251
"Volunteer Programs Give Big Payoff" 371
"Volunteer Services at the Cornell Public Library" 26
"Volunteer Services for Schools; National School Volunteer Program" 45
"Volunteer Services System. Handbook 1: Guidebook to a Volunteer Services System" 259
"Volunteer Services System. Handbook 2: Organizing a Volunteer Services System" 260
"Volunteer Services System. Handbook 3: Information System for a Volunteer

Services System"
261
"Volunteer Services
  System. Handbook 4:
  Program Operations"
  262
"Volunteer Services
  System. Handbook 5:
  Volunteer Personnel
  Operations" 263
"Volunteer Services
  System. Handbook 6:
  School Volunteer
  Operations" 264
"Volunteer Services
  System (Third Year
  Report)" 293
*Volunteer Training and
  Development: A
  Manual* 307
"Volunteer Tutorial
  Program: A Guide for
  Administration" 359
"Volunteer Tutorial
  System" 10
"Volunteer Use Up in
  Phoenix" 405
"Volunteer Way, The"
  270
"Volunteer Work--Its
  Relation to
  Education" 14
"Volunteering is In"
  340
"Volunteerism and
  Education" 394
"Volunteerism in Adult
  Education: A
  Guidebook for
  Increasing the Scope
  and Quality of
  Volunteer Programs
  in Adult Education"
  435
"Volunteerism in
  Education:

Translating Spirit
  into State Action"
  391
"Volunteerism in
  Libraries" 364
"Volunteers" 249
"Volunteers: Altruists
  or Prima Donnas?"
  366
"Volunteers and Older
  Students" 380
"Volunteers and the
  Freedom Schools:
  Education for Social
  Change in
  Mississippi" 402
"Volunteers, Another
  View: How Do the
  Volunteers Feel
  about Their Work?"
  341
"Volunteers are 'In'
  ... in the New Haven
  Schools" 389
"Volunteers Assist
  Staffers, Run Area
  Libraries" 354
"Volunteers at
  Providence Library
  Help Staff Handle
  Rising Demand" 429
"Volunteers Can Bring
  the Help You Need"
  236
"Volunteers--For
  Publicity" 12
"Volunteers for the
  Library" 220
"Volunteers in
  Arlington County
  Contribute Hours and
  Know-how" 406
"Volunteers in
  Education" 373
*Volunteers in
  Education: A*

Title Index

Handbook for Coordinators of Volunteer Programs 280
"Volunteers in Education. Fourth Region Workshop Report 1971" 167
"Volunteers in Education: Interim Evaluation Report July 1, 1971-June 30, 1972" 194
"Volunteers in Education: Interim Evaluation Report July 1, 1972-June 30, 1973" 210
"Volunteers in Education: Materials for Volunteer Programs and the Volunteer" 138
Volunteers in Education. Regional VIII Workshop. Summary Report 150
Volunteers in Education. Regional IX Workshop. Summary Report 151
"Volunteers in Libraries" 305
"Volunteers in Libraries" 484
Volunteers in Libraries 330
Volunteers in Libraries II 431
"Volunteers in Libraries: An Untapped Asset?" 168
"Volunteers in Libraries: Guards, PR, Outreach" 328
"Volunteers in Libraries: New and Ongoing Programs" 250
"Volunteers in Libraries: Reports From All Over" 407
"Volunteers in Public Libraries: The Costs and Benefits" 393
"Volunteers in Public Schools: A Pilot Project in Georgia" 207
"Volunteers in Reading (December 1977 issue of *Reporting on Reading*) 329
"Volunteers in the Chapel Hill Public Library" 229
"Volunteers in the Classroom" 231
Volunteers in the Lancaster County Library 209
"Volunteers in the Public School: Bonus or Burden?" 75
"Volunteers in the Schools: A Gift of Service" 352
"Volunteers in the Schools: A Positive Approach to Schooling" 487
"Volunteers in the Secondary Schools: A Valuable Resource" 381
"Volunteers Keep an Adult Basic Education Tutoring Program VITAL" 397

"Volunteers Offer Library Services to Shut-Ins" 301
"Volunteers Sought for Literacy Drive" 30
"Volunteers to Help Individuals" 114
"Volunteers--Worth Their Weight in Gold" 384
"Volunteers? Yes!" 299
"Washington University Campus Y Tutoring Project, The" 31
"Welcome Volunteers: Parents: An Asset" 226
"What Price Parent Participation?" 13
"What's Happening in Education? Teachers Aides" 4
"When Migrant Children Arrive ... Volunteers are There to Help" 11
"When a Student Needs a Friend Is When Teachers in Winnetka, Illinois, Turn to Their Pool of School Volunteers" 110
"Where Student Activists are VIP's" 111
"Who Was That Stranger I Saw in Your Classroom?" 73
"Why Johnny's Mother Still Can't Read" 493
"Winnetka 'Idea' Reaches Out" 96

Working with Children Individually: A Handbook for School Volunteers and Auxiliary Staff 59
"Year of Turmoil: Threats to Budgets, Volatile Network and Utility Fortunes, Fast-spreading Automation, and an Acute Concern for Priorities, A" 398
You Can Remake America 106
"Your Volunteer Program: Organization and Administration of Volunteer Programs" 136
"Youthful Revolution in Puddledock, The" 55

SUBJECT INDEX

Adult Education 15,
54, 123, 124, 126,
160, 182, 186, 199,
223, 232, 273, 337,
339, 361, 362, 397,
411, 414, 417, 430,
432, 434, 435, 444,
445, 453, 455, 468,
483
Adult Education Act
445
Adult Literacy
Initiative 472
After-school programs
28, 29, 37, 81, 83,
119, 454
Alabama 186
Altrusa Club 396
American Association
of University Women
11, 52
American Indians 123
American Library
Association 322,
385
Appalachia 177, 186,
242
Arizona 95, 381, 405,
435, 461
Baylor Literacy Center
6
Blacks, as recipients
of volunteer
services 22, 27,
31, 90, 100, 131,
224, 316, 462, 475;
as volunteers 10,
36, 103, 106, 108,
475
Boy Scouts 378, 396
Budget constraints, in
adult education
445, 455; in higher
education 478; in
libraries 161, 196,
229, 304, 351, 358,
366, 368, 393, 409,
431; in schools 9,
11, 31, 32, 39, 75,
93, 95, 125, 166,
184, 221, 248, 252,
272, 279, 282, 313,
340, 369, 371, 374,
375, 387, 392, 485
Business support 204,
335, 387, 421, 448
California 9, 34, 67,
84, 88, 117, 119,
125, 196, 215, 221,
284, 298, 303, 318,
351, 368, 371, 374,
392, 426, 457, 463,
475, 490; Los
Angeles 86, 103,
129, 138, 211, 212,
221, 223, 236, 265,
301, 413
Chicago *See* Illinois
Classism, volunteer
work's role in
overcoming 127
Coalition for Literacy
385
College professors as
volunteers 348
College students as
volunteers 1, 10,
22, 27, 31, 36, 38,
44, 58, 79, 90, 92,
100, 111, 154, 169,
197, 363, 428
Colorado 215, 221
Community Involvement
190, 201, 212, 310,
314, 317, 325, 334,
440 *Also see* Public
relations,
publicity.
Compensatory education
See Disadvantaged
persons

143

Computers, as teaching
aids 446, 477, 494;
replacing volunteers
480
Connecticut 32, 142,
178, 179, 235, 236,
299, 389
Coordinators (of
volunteers) 142,
163, 176, 187, 230,
280, 339, 404, 444
Costs associated with
volunteer programs
157, 225, 240, 349
Council of Jewish
Women 12
Desegregation 146,
360, 380 *Also see*
Racism
Disadvantaged persons
28, 34, 37, 43, 94,
122, 155, 242, 370,
376
Early Childhood
Education 416
Early Childhood
Education Act 321
Elderly persons as
volunteers *See*
Older volunteers
Elementary and
Secondary Education
Act 68, 165, 187,
220, 274, 370
Exploitive nature of
volunteer work 364
Fathers 68, 84, 89,
172, 255, 277, 387
The Feminine Mystique
62
Florida 219, 317,
318, 347, 403, 466;
Dade County 143,
144, 145, 146, 147,
148, 149, 159, 180,
205, 224, 233, 270,
340, 361
Ford Foundation 53
Freedom Schools
(Mississippi) 402
Fundraising 412, 430
Future Teachers Club
29, 80
Georgia 207
Government
encouragement of
volunteers 59, 198,
207, 278, 287, 360,
391, 394, 401, 403,
433, 486 *Also see*
Elementary and
Secondary Education
Act, Head Start,
Library Services and
Construction Act, U.
S. Office of
Education.
Government funding,
need for 16, 276,
278, 329, 391, 428,
459, 464, 469, 493
Grandmothers 51, 89
Head Start 51, 129,
164, 241, 420, 425
High-school students
3, 9, 22, 170, 222,
269, 423
Higher education,
volunteers in 258,
344, 355, 356, 455,
478
Hispanics 11, 37,
103, 123, 129, 159,
224
Homemakers *See*
Mothers; Wives
Hospitals 435, 478
Idaho 221, 268
Illinois 11, 35, 96,
110, 121, 184, 296,
424, 439, 473;

Subject Index

Chicago 22, 28, 83,
  141, 376, 441
Indiana 369, 386, 397
Junior League 12, 52,
  142, 178, 275
Key Club 29
Kiwanis Club 432
Laubach 30, 357, 457
Legal issues 315,
  320, 347, 420
Librarians 362, 364
Libraries, volunteers
  in 7, 15, 25, 26,
  32, 41, 42, 49, 54,
  61, 81, 87, 89, 141,
  162, 168, 177, 185,
  192, 196, 202, 209,
  220, 229, 239, 249,
  250, 251, 265, 272,
  285, 286, 289, 291,
  298, 300, 301, 302,
  303, 304, 305, 306,
  308, 309, 322, 328,
  342, 343, 354, 358,
  366, 368, 382, 386,
  388, 390, 393, 398,
  406, 407, 408, 410,
  411, 413, 424, 426,
  429, 431, 436, 439,
  447, 452, 457, 473,
  480, 481, 482, 484,
  485, 486, 490, 492,
  494
Library Services and
  Construction Act
  386, 395, 397, 457
Literacy Council 33,
  57, 174, 414
Literacy Volunteers of
  America, Inc. 118,
  235, 273, 291, 292,
  372, 387, 417, 457,
  482
Los Angeles *See*
  California
Louisiana 12, 381

Lutheran Church Women
  446
Male volunteers 8,
  10, 29, 35, 37, 52,
  108, 110, 115, 211,
  288, 327, 376, 378,
  402, 424, 437, 475
  Also see Fathers,
  Parents
Management of
  volunteers 188,
  193, 194, 202, 203,
  208, 225, 230, 233,
  236, 245, 259, 260,
  261, 262, 263, 264,
  267, 271, 280, 284,
  290, 293, 294, 307,
  310, 314, 330, 342,
  359, 366, 377, 419,
  431, 437, 444, 458
Maryland 3, 267, 390,
  395, 401, 437, 494
Massachusetts 85,
  156, 235; Boston
  117, 127, 138, 236
Mayor's Commission on
  Literacy
  (Philadelphia) 447,
  462
Media centers,
  volunteers in 297,
  299, 303, 341, 423
Mexican-Americans *See*
  Hispanics
Michigan 191, 282,
  287, 326, 345, 454;
  Detroit 138, 165,
  298
Minnesota 64, 49, 92
Mississippi 402
Missouri 31, 194,
  215, 325
Montana 126
Mothers 5, 25, 32,
  42, 51, 62, 66, 74,
  76, 77, 89, 95, 122,

129, 132, 133, 136,
137, 139, 154, 200,
255, 256, 266, 275,
284, 285, 325, 326,
333, 379, 383, 387,
393, 450, 470, 493
Also see Parents
National Affiliation
  for Literacy Advance
  181, 372, 456
National Council of
  Negro Women 250
National Honor Society
  23
National Organization
  for Women 239, 250,
  307, 329
National School Public
  Relations
  Association 206
National School
  Volunteer Program
  45, 270, 318, 332,
  399, 489
Nebraska 199
New Hampshire 221
New Jersey 29, 108,
  199, 320
New York 5, 8, 13,
  71, 75, 114, 235,
  237, 251, 305, 381,
  427; New York City
  20, 21, 60, 171,
  258, 485
North Carolina 54,
  187, 229, 419
Northern Student
  Movement 27
Ohio 138, 189, 190,
  199, 230, 479
Oklahoma 381
Older volunteers 94,
  96, 154, 156, 164,
  243, 244, 274, 281,
  287, 306, 327, 338,
  345, 355, 356, 357,

365, 374, 379, 383,
387, 392, 399, 401,
415, 416, 422, 425,
437, 451, 454, 461,
463, 469, 476, 492
Opposition to
  volunteers 48, 182,
  187, 195, 202, 225,
  227, 231, 234, 242,
  266, 289, 296, 298,
  305, 311, 314, 327,
  337, 339, 352, 354,
  364, 398, 409, 419
Oregon 99, 135, 388,
  470
Parent-Teacher
  Association 42, 184
Parents 2, 4, 8, 13,
  73, 82, 112, 115,
  134, 213, 220, 226,
  227, 279, 311, 312,
  317, 321, 370, 383,
  421, 477
Pennsylvania 209,
  324, 432;
  Philadelphia 117,
  138, 244, 447, 462
Political nature of
  volunteer work 471,
  489
Principals (school)
  213, 336, 487
Private sector *See*
  Business support
Professionalism 442,
  449
Project Upswing 248,
  253
Public **Relations**,
  Publicity 214, 221
  Also see Community
  involvement
Racism, volunteer
  work's role in
  overcoming 85, 107,
  127

RAISE (Retirees Active in Student Education) 454
RSVP (Retired Senior Volunteer Program) 237, 324, 438 *Also see* Older volunteers
Rhode Island 157, 276, 400, 429
Right to Read, The (program) 113, 130, 159, 198, 232, 245, 247, 282, 335, 449
Senior citizens *See* Older volunteers
Sexism, volunteer work's role in overcoming 85
Southern United States 17, 316 *Also see* specific Southern states by name
South Carolina 359, 476
South Dakota 381
Statistical information *See* Surveys
Students as volunteers 14, 18, 19, 22, 23, 39, 47, 50, 55, 67, 68, 70, 72, 80, 85, 91, 99, 101, 107, 116, 217, 238, 288, 410, 469, 477
Surveys 119, 295, 315, 317, 333; of literacy programs 491; of schools 71, 135, 210, 325; of students as recipients of volunteer services 102; of teachers 63, 78, 105, 466; of volunteer coordinators 404; of volunteers 33, 57, 78, 98, 102, 109, 254, 341, 466
Tax advantages 241
Teacher aides 4, 19, 51, 56, 58, 63, 68, 71, 76, 82, 105, 112, 115, 120, 135, 154, 172, 173, 175, 219, 228, 234, 274, 277, 323, 334
Teachers 124, 158, 219, 231, 319, 323, 466; as managers of volunteers 65, 72, 86, 101, 149, 226, 277, 311, 350, 379, 443, 458, 472
Tennessee 295, 357
Texas 6, 41, 185, 232, 275, 418, 460, 489
Training 97, 118, 129, 138, 139, 142, 144, 174, 183, 207, 215, 216, 273, 307, 318, 319, 331, 365, 384, 474; volunteer work as training for paid employment 140, 289, 367, 423
Tutors, tutoring 10, 19, 22, 23, 27, 30, 31, 40, 44, 46, 50, 61, 67, 72, 80, 91, 99, 102, 103, 104, 107, 116, 118, 120, 124, 131, 139, 142, 148, 152, 153, 160, 171, 175, 178, 179, 183, 197, 215, 216, 218, 222, 224, 235, 238, 244, 246, 247, 299, 316, 357, 372, 376, 408, 411, 414,

428, 432, 441, 442,
449, 461, 465, 467,
475, 477, 481, 486,
489, 490
Underfunding *See*
   Budget constraints
U. S. Office of
   Education 83, 98,
   130
Value of volunteer
   services 199, 359,
   369, 418, 426
Virginia 381, 393,
   417
VISTA 81, 456
VITAL (Volunteers In
   Tutoring Adult
   Learners 386, 397
Volunteer teachers 6,
   320, 346, 353, 434
Washington, D.C. 33,
   40, 57, 81, 98
Washington (state)
   135, 197, 454
West Virginia 494
Wisconsin 131, 407,
   410
Wives 26, 51, 75,
   100, 108, 177, 180,
   182, 184, 229, 479
Wyoming 396
YWCA 52
Youth Tutoring Youth
   217

APR 0 1 1991